# Appreciative Inquiry

## A Positive Approach to Building Cooperative Capacity

**Frank J. Barrett, Ph.D.**
and
**Ronald E. Fry, Ph.D.**

Taos Institute Publications
Chagrin Falls, Ohio

# APPRECIATIVE INQUIRY

Cover design by Jamieson Fry

Special thanks to Richard Doyle
for proofreading and editing earlier versions of this book.

SECOND PRINTING 2008

FIRST EDITION
Copyright © 2005
by Frank J. Barrett and Ronald E. Fry

Library of Congress Catalog Card Number: 2005935499

ISBN-13: 978-0-7880-2163-3
ISBN-10: 0-7880-2163-X

PRINTED IN U.S.A.

# Introduction To
# Taos Institute Publications

The Taos Institute is a nonprofit organization dedicated to the development of social constructionist theory and practices for purposes of world benefit. Constructionist theory and practice locate the source of meaning, value, and action in communicative relations among people. Chief importance is placed on relational process and its outcomes for the welfare of all. Taos Institute Publications offers contributions to cutting-edge theory and practice in social construction. These books are designed for scholars, practitioners, students, and the openly curious. The **Focus Book Series** provides brief introductions and overviews that illuminate theories, concepts, and useful practices. The **Books for Professionals Series** provides in-depth works, which focus on recent developments in theory and practice. Books in both series are particularly relevant to social scientists and to practitioners concerned with individual, family, organizational, community, and societal change.

Kenneth J. Gergen
President, Board of Directors
The Taos Institute

For information about the Taos Institute visit: www.taosinstitute.net

# Taos Institute Publications

## Focus Book Series

*The Appreciative Organization*, (2001) by Harlene Anderson, David Cooperrider, Kenneth J. Gergen, Mary Gergen, Sheila McNamee, and Diana Whitney

*Appreciative Leaders: In the Eye of the Beholder*, (2001) Edited by Marge Schiller, Bea Mah Holland, and Deanna Riley

*Experience AI: A Practitioner's Guide to Integrating Appreciative Inquiry and Experiential Learning*, (2001) by Miriam Ricketts and Jim Willis

*Appreciative Sharing of Knowledge: Leveraging Knowledge Management for Strategic Change*, (2004) by Tojo Thatchekery

*Social Construction: Entering the Dialogue,* (2004) by Kenneth J. Gergen and Mary Gergen

*Dynamic Relationships: Unleashing the Power of Appreciative Inquiry in Daily Living*, (2005) by Jacqueline M. Stavros and Cheri B. Torres

*Appreciative Inquiry: A Positive Approach to Building Cooperative Capacity*, (2005) by Frank J. Barrett, Ph.D. and Ronald E. Fry

## Books for Professionals Series

*SocioDynamic Counselling: A Practical Guide to Meaning Making*, (2004) by R. Vance Peavy

*Experiential Exercises in Social Construction – A Fieldbook for Creating Change*, (2004) by Robert Cottor, Alan Asher, Judith Levin, and Cindy Weiser

*Dialogues About a New Psychology,* (2004) by Jan Smedslund

*Therapeutic Realities: Social Construction and the Therapeutic Process*, (2005) by Kenneth J. Gergen

For on-line ordering of books from Taos Institute Publications visit www.taospub.net or www.taosinstitute.net/publishing/publishing.html

For further information, write or call:
1-888-999-TAOS, 1-440-338-6733, info@taosinstitute.net or
taosinstitutepublishing@alltel.net

# Editors' Note

Dear Readers:

*Appreciative Inquiry: A Positive Approach to Building Cooperative Capacity* is a significant offering by Taos Institute Publishing because it offers both new learners about AI and those who are already practitioners of AI the opportunity to see that the core of AI is about *capacity building*—something significant to the success of every organization.

As you will read in this book, this strength-based approach to cooperative capacity building starts with the very first question—an unconditional positive question—that moves the organization into the direction of its questions. To increase an organization's capacity to learn, there are three in depth case studies offered by the authors: Roadway 211, "Medic Inn," and the Navy's use of AI. Roadway 211 has used AI diligently in its efforts to become carrier of choice. One of the first in-depth applications of AI during its development was at Medic Inn, discussed in the book in an effort to link to AI's origins as a process that makes capacity building possible. Lastly, the process at the US Navy is intriguing. As some might say, "If AI can be used successfully in the command-and-control oriented military system, it can work anywhere."

Barrett and Fry feel the legacy of inquiry is the igniting of cooperative capacity that transforms. They offer us their own "experience-based belief that AI is a means to inquire into what cooperative capacity is so that we can understand what triggers capacity building." If you have a hunger to learn about Appreciative Inquiry—or if you want an easily consumed book on AI for a client, this book is for you.

Sincerely,
Jane Galloway Seiling and Jackie Stavros, Editors
The Taos Institute Focus Book Series

*To Mary Hagan Barrett — who taught me about the power of appreciation and resilience; and to my friend, Bob Rink, who deeply knows the meaning of blessing.*

Frank J. Barrett

*To Maureen, Jamieson, and Justin; you continue to awaken my attention to what I most appreciate in life.*

Ronald Fry

# Table Of Contents

# Foreword

Within these pages is a simple yet revolutionary philosophy of organizational learning and change: discover everything that "gives life" to the cooperative capacity of a human system—and then let go.

What gets co-constructed thereafter will be anything but linear. Like jazz improvisation or a creative jam session, it will literally be impossible to predict the emerging new opportunities, options, and shared possibilities. But one thing is almost certain: whatever gets created will be good. It will be valued *and valuable* to the human system for one overarching reason: the quality of the "relational space" from which the new constructions of the future are nurtured makes a difference that makes the difference.

Relationships, propose the authors of this wonderful introduction to Appreciative Inquiry, come alive where there is an *appreciative* question, when there is a deliberate search for the good and the best in one another; and in human systems the process of studying a phenomenon actually changes that phenomenon, in effect creating a new reality during the process of inquiry. That's what this book is all about. It is all about power of "AI" as a way of creating a relational space for the cooperative construction of reality.

Based on almost twenty years of field research in organizations like the United States Navy, Roadway Express, and Nokia as well as years of scholarly commitment to social constructionist approaches to human science inquiry, the authors of this book finally put into print a pragmatic, inspiring, and simple account of an approach to strength-based change that has elevated the capacities of thousands of businesses, change leaders, and teams to realize their enormous potentials. It's the kind of focus book that people will want to hand out at the front end of a major organization-wide change initiative. And it is a perfect companion piece for workshops, foundation courses on AI, and leadership programs.

Frank Barrett, a former jazz musician and now Professor of management at the US Naval Postgraduate School, and Professor Ron Fry, the Director of what is perhaps the most acclaimed Masters degree program in the country in positive organization development at Case Western Reserve University, have been pioneers in the appreciative inquiry movement since its earliest days. They are two of my treasured colleagues and closest friends—and along with Suresh Srivastva, Diana Whitney, Jane Watkins, Jim Ludema, and Ken Gergen they have done more to develop new understandings of how and why appreciative inquiry works than anyone else in the field. What is their core proposition? In Barrett and Fry's words it is this: *"Cooperative capacity is fostered through an appreciative declaration of faith in the potential goodness of human groups and organization."* Cooperative capacity is the secret, they demonstrate, to achieving superior results in the change arena.

This is a Taos Institute *Focus Book* that is both substantive and accessible in a "how to" way with its stories from the field, practical tips, and its challenges to long-accepted myths about change. In my view this is a special volume that will at once captivate, guide and reassure, and enlighten, as it dramatically transforms the way you lead change in your organizations, your family or community, and your future.

David L. Cooperrider
Case Western Reserve University
July 28, 2005

**Prologue**

# Building Capacity
# Through Asking Questions

Organizations study things all the time. It seems there are always challenges and opportunities that demand a task force, a team of consultants, or an ad hoc group to diagnose some problem or conduct some study. These studies are, in part, occasions for learning. Sometimes it is simply a matter of taking a snapshot of a situation. Other times it's a matter of systematically digging down to understand the root causes behind a troubling trend. Why is turnover so high over the last three years? Why is employee morale so low? How has organizational climate changed since the last restructuring? What do we need to do to get higher returns? How do we improve quality and customer satisfaction? But the problems to be solved and the crises to be managed all begin with the questions that managers ask. *This may strike you as trivial, but the questions we ask determine whether we eventually diminish our capacity to grow and develop, or increase it.*

Consider this example. In one organization executives were alarmed by the high rate of employee turnover. Fifteen percent of the workforce was leaving after two years. Management launched a discussion of the high turnover rate and decided to commission a study. When they met to discuss the findings, they discovered a long list of complaints and concerns: salary was too low; bonuses were unpredictable; the work environment was stressful; task demands were excessive; managers were more concerned with punishing failure than rewarding success; employees felt their input was not valued; and so on. The discussion soon revealed disagreements about the roots of these problems, followed by finger pointing and some sharp exchanges. Some defended their roles and insisted that the fault was elsewhere. Finally, an external consultant asked a different question: what is it about this company that makes the other 85 percent of employees want to stay? After a momentary silence, one manager said that there was no reason to ask that question because it was not the 85% that was causing them to be concerned. Then another suggested that they at least try to identify the reasons that people stayed at the firm. They decided to ask a sample of employees about their attraction to the firm—for example, what was it they liked about working there and what were some of their positive work experiences? The study uncovered hundreds of surprisingly positive stories, many of which revealed factors that most executives had forgotten or hadn't even considered. They began to see moments of inter-departmental collaboration, times when employees were empowered to come up with creative solutions and examples of bold and inclusive decision making.

At the next meeting of the Executive Board, participants held an entirely different conversation. They talked about the strengths of the firm, the unique identity of the culture, and the ways that they could expand opportunities for employees to collaborate and experiment with participative decision making. They began to consider new strategies that could lead to previously unimagined breakthroughs. They learned to pay closer attention to what they were doing well, to the practices that drew people to the firm and compelled them to stay. Their entire approach shifted from fixing what they saw as problems to enhancing what they now realized were their core strengths.

This example demonstrates a critical aspect of questions, that is, they can be so pervasive that we rarely think about them. Managers are always asking questions, ranging from simple wonderings to full-scale inquiries. This is as it should be, since questions are at the root of all learning and therefore the key in the development of any team, organization or system. In this book we argue that it is worth paying attention to how we ask questions because *the asking of questions already begins to transform and change the capacity of the human system we seek to understand.*

Now of course, it's not enough to just ask good questions. It's also important to pay attention to the data that questions generate.

Consider the example that Jim Collins recounts.[1] He compared the development of two competing organizations in the same industry—A&P and Kroger supermarkets. Both organizations asked, what is it that customers want from their local grocery store? How can we provide products and services that will keep customers returning to our grocery stores? The difference was that when Kroger asked what drew customers to certain stores over others, they paid attention to what they heard and made sure that they grew in that direction. This was a case where two organizations asked good questions—what is it that delights the customer? One acted on the data and the other didn't. As Collins contends, one of the characteristics of great organizations is that they ask the right questions *and* they pay attention to the results even if the answers imply the need for simple or radical changes. We agree.

Learning always begins with a question; a moment of inquiry. These questions represent attempts to learn that often result in efforts to improve performance, or to better a situation in some way. It is worth reflecting upon the way that managers form the questions that create openings for new understandings of situations. *This is a book about framing questions with a positive stance and focusing on topics that enhance organizational learning which results in increased cooperative capacity.*

**Two Different Approaches to Improving Performance**.
The way we begin these moments of inquiry is all-important. We wish to share two provocative examples of contrasting approaches to learning and capacity building. The first occurs during the US Presidential Campaign of 2000. After the first Gore-Bush debate, some observers remarked that Al Gore was aggressive and unrelenting; some even called him dogmatic. After this debate, a popular television show, Saturday Night Live, parodied the two politicians. In particular, they mocked Gore's aggressiveness and unrelenting repetition of the word "lockbox" in reference to protecting social security.

What is interesting, for our purposes, is how Gore set about improving his performance in preparation for the second debate with George W. Bush. Did he think about his strengths, his areas of competence and seek ways to build on them? Apparently not. Rather, he took a more common approach—seeking to discover his mistakes and work on them to improve his performance. And he had help. Gore's staff showed him a tape of the Saturday Night Live skit a few days before the second debate. The actor depicting Al Gore, Darrell Hammond, imitated Gore's Tennessee twang and played Gore as a pompous, condescending, "know it all" buffoon who sounded like he was talking to kindergartners; he frequently uttered exasperated sighs while the actor depicting Bush answered questions. After aides showed him a tape of the skit, he was motivated to change his approach and was heard to pledge, "a few less sighs, absolutely."

No doubt with this image in mind, in the second debate Gore was focused on not making the same mistakes. In fact, he was noticeably more reticent and withdrawn; more polite, less decisive, and less willing to challenge Bush. The image of Hammond's exaggerated parody from Saturday Night Live may well have guided his presentation of himself in the second debate. He was concerned, we assume, to not be seen as pompous or arrogant. He was cautious and understated. It's unlikely that we will ever know for sure what went through his mind, but we do know that the outcome was not positive for him. Many said later that the second debate was a turning point and gave Bush much needed momentum. President Clinton, watching Gore's performance in the second debate, reportedly wondered aloud why Gore was so listless. Meanwhile, one of Bush's aides told him afterward that he had just won the election.

We present this vignette because it illustrates that a problem-solving approach to learning can have debilitating effects. Al Gore did what many of us do instinctively. It seems common sense that if we want to get better, if we want to improve some capacity to perform, then we would do well to study our errors and fix them.

Contrast this with a different story of learning and capacity building. Here we cite the example from a very different era and very different context. In 1501, Michelangelo was commissioned to create a marble statue of David for a cathedral in Florence. He carved it from a piece of marble that a previous sculptor, Agostino di Duccio, had worked with, but discarded 40 years earlier out of frustration. What is most interesting, for our purposes, was Michelangelo's mindset and how he set about to perform his formidable task. Carving a complex figure from a resistant material demands strong problem-solving skills.[2]

But the artist did not approach his task as solving a problem. Michelangelo said that when he looked at the discarded marble, he saw David already there in his full, pristine pose. What was needed, he said, was simply to "clear the rest of the marble away in order to bring David out." Michelangelo's primary concern, his most vital energy, was devoted to forming an image of the perfect David before he ever put chisel to stone.

Critics and observers are still in awe of Michelangelo's David. It was carved, according to Paul Johnson, "with almost atrocious skill and energy."[3] We are in awe of his mindset. Looking at the same piece of stone discarded by an earlier artist—presumably out of frustration—Michelangelo could see the David waiting to be realized from within the marble. His *capacity* to imagine David in his pristine wholeness, is an approach to learning that leads to bold innovation. (Later, by the way, the statue was seen as such a radical artistic achievement that it came to symbolize the identity of the community of Florence. Rather than placing it in the cathedral, it was put in a more public display in front of the town hall, the Palazzo Vecchio).

These vignettes illustrate two different approaches to improving performance that begin with two different questions; two different topics of inquiry. One is a *deficit* orientation leading to problem solving; the other a positive, *appreciative* orientation leading to increased capacity and innovation. They hold many lessons for managers and leaders of organizational change. Al Gore was fixated on not making mistakes; Michelangelo was consumed with forming a perfect image of David and extracting it from the marble mass. Think about the questions that consumed both of these figures. Gore probably asked himself several times: how can I make sure that I'm not too overbearing? Then imagine the question that guided Michelangelo: how can I craft this beautiful image for all to see from this mass of marble?

**Inquiry and Capacity Building**
There is another important distinction to be drawn from these two stories of performance improvement. One is a story of "getting better" and the other is a story of "capacity building" or expansion of one's ability in the pursuit of excellence. All improvement is not capacity building. As we will see, the dynamics of expanding one's capacity to act are different from those associated with fixing, repairing, or healing. The Appreciative Inquiry (AI) approach to capacity building described in this book is unique from other change philosophies in that it focuses on developing organizations from a strength-based perspective.

The significance of this emphasis is illustrated by the continuum in Figure 1 below which is adapted from the work of Cameron, Dutton, and Quinn in the emerging field of Positive Organization Scholarship.[4] The left end of the continuum represents human systems that are in a poor state of health, where organizations act irresponsibly, perform poorly, or produce low quality. The center point represents an average, normative state, where social systems enact a minimum standard of ethics, have average performance, or produce at least a minimal level of quality. The right end of the continuum represents a state of high ethics and social responsibility, exceptional and enduring performance, or flawless quality. The social forces in most human systems have a normative momentum that tends to move behaviors, attitudes, and actions toward the center. "Fixing things" are the dynamics of a shift from low to average performance and are qualitatively different from those that "build capacity to excel and flourish" by shifting an organization from, as Jim Collins calls it, "good to great."

**Figure 1. The Dynamics of Capacity Building**

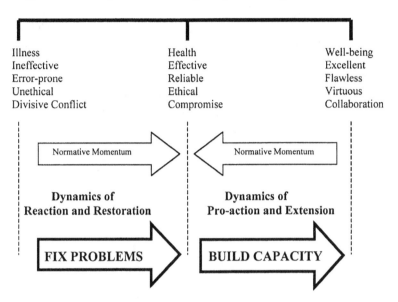

| Illness | Health | Well-being |
| Ineffective | Effective | Excellent |
| Error-prone | Reliable | Flawless |
| Unethical | Ethical | Virtuous |
| Divisive Conflict | Compromise | Collaboration |

Normative Momentum | Normative Momentum

**Dynamics of
Reaction and Restoration** | **Dynamics of
Pro-action and Extension**

**FIX PROBLEMS** | **BUILD CAPACITY**

Traditional Organization Development techniques, with a focus on diagnosis and problem-solving, are centrally concerned with fixing poor performance—with healing. Problem-centric techniques typically unfold through discovering a symptom, performing an analysis of causes and problems, analyzing the problems, developing possible solutions, and then creating a treatment. The underlying metaphor is that the organization is ill and that the manager or consultant is a physician whose purpose is to generate a healing prescription. In contrast, AI squarely focuses on generating dynamics that will shift organizations from the average to the exceptional. It is assumed that a basic level of normal function exists in any organization, and that the potential— or capacity—for exceptional performance is already embedded within the organization. *Thus capacity building, for us, is the process of elaborating and expanding on a system's strengths—usually closely tied to cooperative acts—in order to move that system from good to great, from*

*doing well to always winning, from constantly correcting to for-*
*ever innovating, and so on.*

We are calling attention here to the contrast between a deficit approach to learning (that is, I intend to avoid doing what I did before), and an appreciative approach (I intend to create this wonderful image of David from raw material). Our point is this: There is little capacity for creativity and innovation when one is overly concerned with avoiding mistakes or repairing something. Michelangelo was able to create a positive image of what he desired; Gore focused on what he wanted to avoid. That difference is everything.

**FOCUS BOX**

This book is devoted to exploring more fully the lessons from Michelangelo's approach to the creation of David—an appreciative approach to capacity building. We want to explore more deeply the consequences of starting any innovation or change journey with a different question: how can we generate a vivid image of the world we most desire? As we will see throughout this book, this strength-based approach to capacity building starts with the very first question; a small move that has large consequences.

**Chapter 1**

# The Quick Introduction

As noted in the Prologue, the purpose of this book is to provide a concise introduction to, and overview of, the growing discipline and practice of Appreciative Inquiry (AI) as an approach to organizational capacity building. Although writings to date on AI have not emphasized its use in "building cooperative capacity," it is our belief that this is a potential outcome from using AI. Also, while the number of texts, handbooks, and case studies on AI are expanding, we feel there is a strong call for a "quick read" that will assist curious learners, change agents, or leaders in determining if they are interested in learning more about this rapidly growing field of theory and practice. If you are intrigued by the prospect of mobilizing rapid, positive change through increased cooperation among multiple stakeholders in a human system that is important to you, read on.

The AI approach is a way of being...as a leader, a parent, a colleague, a partner, a change agent, a team leader, a project manager, a teacher, employer, or employee. It is an exciting and energizing way to approach individual, team, organization, community, and global renewal and transformation. While it is not *the* only answer to the current challenges and need for transformative cooperation we face, it is *a* promising approach.

You can read this book from beginning to end or go to specific parts that most interest you. In the next part, Chapter 2, we provide some basic definitions and assertions about what Appreciative Inquiry stands for—in theory and in practice. Chapter 3 will support our claim that Appreciative Inquiry is here, growing in popularity and usage, for a reason: our socialized tendency to engage in deficit discourse—about anything—is keeping us from being creative, innovative, and collaborative in the corporate and social arenas that most need renewal or transformation. Some of the underlying logic or theory that provides a foundation for this exciting practice is covered in Chapters 4 and 5. Chapters 6 and 7 will guide you through the steps of an appreciative inquiry process to help you get a feel for the key activities and outcomes along the way. Chapters 8 and 9 provide practical examples of AI in use to develop team and organizational capacity. Finally, in Chapter 10, we end with some reflections on how AI is transforming the way we think about and organize for positive change.

We have tried to write just as we talk and share our experiences from our work with AI, as if we were in one of our workshops, seminars, or systems where we have been privileged to practice this compelling approach to change. We are passionate and principled about this approach to organizational development and transformation and wish for those of you who are truly curious to have this as a first source to refer to in your discovery and learning journey.

Finally, we are not *the* experts. Much of what appears in this short book has been written in various forms by us and numerous colleagues in other places (see Selected References). Here we are attempting to collect and condense a growing body of literature to give those who may be curious or vaguely interested a "taste" of AI in order to see if they want to learn more. We are keen to expand the knowledge and practice of appreciative methods for developing and expanding the cooperative capacity of human systems. In pursuit of this aim, we are indebted to our friend and colleague, David Cooperrider, the first to articulate the AI methodology and theory in his doctoral dissertation and in a subsequent seminal article with Suresh Srivastva. From that beginning, David has worked selflessly to avoid trademarks and patents in order to make learning and discoveries about AI accessible to as many as possible. As members of a small group of faculty and students who worked with David at that creative time, and continue to work and write with him today, we hope this book enhances the accessibility of AI and stimulates more people to embrace this strength-based approach to personal and organizational development in concert with David's vision and passion.

**Chapter 2**

# What Is Appreciative Inqury?

Appreciative Inquiry (AI) is a strength-based, capacity building approach to transforming human systems toward a shared image of their most positive potential by first discovering the very best in their shared experience. It is not about implementing a change to get somewhere; it is about chang*ing*...convening, conversing, and relating with each another in order to tap into the natural capacity for cooperation and change that is in *every* system. At its core, AI is an invitation for members of a system to enhance the generative capacity of dialogue and to attend to the ways that our conversations, particularly our metaphors and stories, facilitate action that support members' highest values and potential. An AI effort seeks to create metaphors, stories, and generative conversations that break the hammerlock of the status quo and open up new vistas that further activities in support of the highest human values and aspirations. AI has distinctive characteristics that expand and strengthen the cooperative capacity of those engaged in this approach.

- *AI is strength-based.* An AI approach begins with the assumption that every human system already has strengths; key features of health and well being (as opposed to needs, diseases, problems and gaps). To identify and nurture that health and well being, AI initiates a deliberate, systematic search for those distinctive assets, best practices, metaphors, dreams, musings, and wishes that embrace a spirit of vitality and potency. It involves searching for the antecedents, catalysts, and supporting factors that embolden and promote an enduring spirit — the central strengths and competencies that contribute to the exceptional potential and vitality of the system. As our experiences are increasingly demonstrating, beginning with a strength-based approach accelerates learning and furthers innovation.

- *AI is an artful search.* The "art of appreciation" is the art of discovering and valuing those factors that give life to any organization or group. Primarily through interviewing and storytelling, the best of the past is discovered to set the stage for effective imagining of what could be. AI searches for the best of "what is" (one's experience up to now) to provide the basis for imagining "what might be." The aim is to generate new knowledge that expands the "realm of the possible" and to help members of an organization envision together a desired future. Such "futures," generated from hopeful, anticipatory images, and linked to actual experiences of being at one's best, are naturally compelling and attractive. Positive future images attract energy and mobilize intention. When guided by hopeful images, groups and organizations are drawn towards cooperating to achieve these visions.

- *AI is collaborative in every aspect.* AI is a collaborative effort—people together discover and create that which is healthy, successful, and positive in organizational life. It involves multiple members or stakeholders conversing and working together. It attends to current successes and past strengths by listening for peak experiences, exceptional moments, or intriguing possibilities, all with the aim of discovering what is happening when their system is operating at its best.

- *AI is inclusive.* Appreciative Inquiry invites a widening circle of voices, creating opportunities and forums for surfacing inspirational stories. This voicing of new possibilities and new conversations of hope and inspiration unleashes a vocabulary of positive possibilities that challenges the status quo. While AI is appropriate for dyads, small groups, and divisions, for us, the most exciting current work with AI is happening with groups of hundreds to thousands of participants, representing all stakeholder voices within a system; coming together to co-discover, co-imagine, co-create, and cooperatively implement positive change.

- *AI is generative.* Any system's imagined future is embedded in the everyday conversations and stories articulated in meetings, hallway discussions, etc. AI fosters a dialogue that cultivates scenarios and theories about what leads to the "good;" to more cooperation, to higher performing work teams, or to higher margins, for example. This generates new words, categories, images, supportive activities, and positive energy to work together. Stories about how the system works at its best—and the emotional experience of connecting around these stories—seed new conversations about the highest ideals, assets, and successes that make positive actions and future collaborations even more possible and desirable. Participants are drawn to work together more toward a common anticipatory image; they seek out more conversation with each other, more ideas for positive change, more involvement from others—they *generate* new possibilities through new or deeper working relationships.

Taken together, these characteristics speak to a capacity building process and the positive potential from engaging in appreciative ways of knowing.

## Summary

Many "high involvement" strategies for organization development have some of the above characteristics, particularly the emphases on collaboration, inclusion, and cooperation. What we believe sets AI apart from other approaches to change is its explicit intent to search from a strengths-only perspective for latent, untapped capacity to pursue shared images of a preferred future. These shared images of what is possible ignite the desire to work together in new ways to co-create that future. In this way, AI becomes generative; it discovers, builds, and expands capacity to cooperate...over and over again.

**FOCUS BOX**

Appreciative Inquiry is a unique way of learning that transforms relationships through its distinctive characteristics. *Artful searching* draws renewed attention to the *strengths* inherent in a relationship, or in a system of relationships, in such a way that *invites* more participants to *cooperate* with each other to create new ways to pursue a positive, shared image of a preferred future—it generates new possibilities.

## Chapter 3

# Why Is AI Important Now?

It seems intuitive that to improve a situation, we need to first fix what is wrong. It makes sense. If someone or something in our organization is broken, the habitual response is to analyze the problem and then fix it. However, we sometimes fail to notice that certain assumptions block the possibility of innovative solutions. Sometimes our questioning is stymied because we are so wedded to a problem-centered view of the world. We just assume that the right thing to do is to first fix the problem.

We have drifted into a "deficiency" perspective of our world. Our vocabulary is loaded with terms that lead us to label and therefore to target the deficient side of human beings and breakdowns in organizations. Martin Seligman, former President of the American Psychological Association, noted in 1998 that over the past thirty years, over 45,000 articles have been published in psychological journals on the topic of depression while less than one percent of that total (about 400) were published on the topic of joy! He described the field of Psychology as having been negative, "essentially for 100 years." He added, "Social science has believed negative things were authentic and human strengths were coping mechanisms."[5]

Few of us are aware of the extent to which a deficit discourse leads us to consider organizations (and people) as a set of problems and managers as (only) expert problem solvers. The once popular TQM movement and now popular Six Sigma programs are, in essence, gap reduction exercises. As Hamel noted,[6]

"The single accomplishment of the industrial age was the notion of continuous improvement. It remains the secular religion of most managers...[and] has reached the point of diminishing returns in incremental improvement programs."

We are not advocating the end of problem-solving. Rather, we warn that if we are not careful, problem-solving may become our "default option" and its overuse can be dangerous for organizations. The implications of this overuse are seldom, if ever, intended by anyone, yet the net results are daunting. The endless pursuit of solutions to problems creates a deficit discourse that has a number of dysfunctional effects in groups and organizations:

- *Fragmentation.* One of the most significant effects of deficit discourse is fragmentation. Because problem-solving begins by breaking complex wholes into small parts, members of organizations become experts in smaller and smaller parts of the situation or context. As expertise develops, managers often become more convinced that their (partial) views of the situation are the right ones, ignoring the larger system context. As a result, they ignore or deny the larger systemic nature of organizational issues.

  Systems theory teaches us that all actions have consequences that are distant in time and space. An approach that seeks to solve isolated problems often causes new problems elsewhere in the system. Analytic problem solving thus fragments the way managers approach issues, shapes the way they ask questions and limits the sources and scope of data they consider. Instead of seeing whole processes, these experts become specialists in sub-processes, using exclusive language that only they and their subgroup understand. Some problems become so familiar and sub-specialized that organizations create whole departments and career tracks around them, leading to further separation between sub-groups.
- *The Invisibility of Possibility.* We often approach problems from the very mind-set that created them in the first place. Accepting the constraints that generated the problem rarely leads to a permanent solution; instead, it often leads to patterns of coping or blaming. People learn to live with diminished expectations, enduring the limitations that generated the very problems that they continue to anticipate. They learn to do what is feasible rather than seeking what is possible.

This is a critical consequence of operating from a problem-solving mentality and risks reaffirming the status quo. The mindset of problem-solving guides the user to the next solution search, driven mainly by criteria of feasibility, based upon past memory, which tends to be a recall of a lot of "not"—what did *not* work, what could *not* be funded, or what the senior management did *not* approve in the past.

- *Self-fulfilling deficit prophesies.* When they lose control and find themselves heading off the road, bicycle riders tend to steer themselves in the direction they look. Consequently, the standard instruction given to them is to avoid looking at the hazards they may encounter in the ditch, and to focus on a course that will keep them on the road. Similarly, human systems move in the direction of their discourse, i.e., what they most talk, and especially, ask questions about.

Consider the case of an automobile repair business that put a premium on customer service, but was unable to reduce a 6-8 percent dissatisfaction rate. They were stuck in a cycle. The more they tried to reduce the 6-8 percent, the more they experienced frustration, finger-pointing, and divisiveness. Upon review of their extensive metrics, it was realized that 99 percent of the measures were questions about customer *dissatisfaction*. Only after putting more emphasis on monitoring and learning about what made their customers *satisfied* were they able to notice small innovations and intriguing solutions that could then be disseminated throughout the organization. With this shift, they eventually were able to achieve their 99% satisfaction target.

- *Over dependence on experts and hierarchy.* Problem-solving rightly respects expertise. However, used repetitively, this mindset encourages a passive dependence by all of the non-experts—that is, most of the organization. Most members rely on a select few "experts," waiting for direction or answers, rather than asking their own questions or proposing their own initiatives. They consider themselves naive. This deference to experts retards the capacity of the system to innovate or execute because "the many" are constantly waiting for "the few" for decisions and initiation. On the plant floor, employees are told to wait for industrial engineers or financial analysts to study a process before any of the operators' suggestions for improvement can be tried. Everyday ideas for improving a process or cooperating with another part of the organization often have to be reviewed first by a select few "decision-makers" higher up in the organization before any action can be taken. These tendencies to wait on "the few" who have more information or decision authority erodes self-confidence in everyone except the experts. The system's capacity for creativity, initiative, and innovative thinking is limited to a handful of individuals who are already overloaded because everyone else is awaiting their decisive inputs.

- *Exhaustion and visionless voice.* Working continuously to fix something or facing an endless list of problems to be solved is exhausting and ultimately stressful. Current research in the field of Positive Psychology shows us very clearly that people under sustained stress and in negative emotional states are less productive, creative, and self-confident. On the other hand, when people experience positive emotion, their attention spans lengthen, they are curious, and they simultaneously hold multiple perspectives.[7] A mindset of curiosity towards multiple perspectives is more likely to trigger insights and inspire innovation.

- *Spirals of separation.* When organizations breakdown, managers are often tempted to find the root of the problem anywhere but in their own units. When inquiry is focused on fixing someone else's problems—combined with the goal of arriving at the one "correct" cause or the one party at fault—people often develop defensive postures, seeking to escape blame, stepping over each other for the honor of being the one who solved the problem. Such defensive moves lead to greater separation between people than the problem itself did, making it difficult to build trust. People become invested in defending their positions, rather than in asking themselves how their thinking is contributing to a solution or desired state. Defensive posturing drives out experimentation and creative thinking. People are more concerned with avoiding blame than with discovering new approaches. We then become more concerned with looking good than in doing well. Managers caught in this defensive spiral become masters of what Argyris[8] called "skilled incompetence"— experts at protecting themselves from the risk of learning and failing, and thus blind to their own need to learn and change. They get better and better at doing the wrong things.

The consequences of these aspects of deficit discourse contribute to a breakdown in relationships, closed-door meetings, and an overall sense of despair. When these kinds of dynamics set in, it should be no surprise to hear that employee cliché: "If it weren't for finding problems and fighting fires, what would managers do? They must come to work looking for problems just to keep busy!" And if we look hard enough for something, we will find it.

To summarize, we have become so locked within a problem-centered, critique-driven worldview that we have severely limited our potential for innovation and transformation. Traditional forms of organizational change have been built upon unquestioned assumptions that constrain the entire change process. Too often change attempts begin from a deficit base, with the assumption that there is something wrong that needs to be fixed. Any solution search founded upon a deficit-oriented view of the world is inherently conservative; it cannot live up to the potential to ignite the collective imagination, to inspire organizational members to create innovative transformations and radical change. Because so much of our daily questioning assumes that there is something wrong in organizations that need to be identified, diagnosed, and fixed, we already begin our efforts with shrunken imaginations.

**FOCUS BOX**

Deficit discourse is everywhere, but its unintended consequences—fragmentation, hopelessness, self-fulfilling deficit views, over dependence on experts or hierarchy, exhaustion and spirals of separation—do not have to envelop us. There is another way to approach everyday life in organizations and social systems. Appreciative Inquiry begins with the assumption that every human system already has assets and positive success experiences. AI is, in essence, a collaborative process for discovering what those strengths are and then using that discovery to imagine, build, and implement a desired future together. It is *not* simply positive thinking or learned optimism. It is a powerful path for change based on creating more cooperative capacity through new kinds of conversations and a special kind of *inquiry*; an intentional way of learning from strengths, not deficits.

**Chapter 4**

# AI's Driving Force:
# The Unconditional Positive Question

New understanding emerges when we begin our capacity building through welcoming *the unknown* as an opportunity for discovery and innovation. It means suspending our confidence in old certainties. This is why the two words—appreciation and inquiry—belong intimately together. It is worth exploring the connection between appreciation and learning that orchestrates opportunities to build cooperative capacity.

The word "appreciate" originates from the Latin word "appretiare" and has four different, but related, meanings. First, "Appretiare" means "*to set a price, to place a value upon, to appraise.*" To appreciate something is to appraise or estimate its worth. We have inherited this way of talking when we say something like "He appreciated the seriousness of the situation." We are saying that he was good at *appraising or placing a value* upon the situation. A second meaning of the word "appretiance" is "*to increase in value,*" in the sense that when someone appreciates an object, *it expands in worth.* When we say that the "value of the house appreciated 15 percent," everyone knows this means that the price increased. Third, "appretiare" can mean *perceiving or seeing.* We have inherited this way of talking as well. If we were to say, "we can appreciate the position you are in," we're not saying we agree with your actions, but we're saying that we can *see your perspective.* The fourth meaning of the term means "*to hold in high estimation, to admire.*" This is the way we use the term when we say "I want to appreciate the work you did on that project." It means that I want to call attention to the positive qualities of your work, your strengths, those things that you did well. These four senses of the term appreciation are each relevant in our treatment of "appreciation" as an activity,.

Taken together, we can see that when we engage by or through appreciation, the world opens up to us in a particular way. Positive qualities and hopeful characteristics become apparent. In this sense, it is fair to say that appreciation is a way of knowing. However, one does not know appreciatively by being a passive observer. Appreciation is a dynamic form of knowledge creation. The act of appreciation is a way of seeing that increases the value of something. As these definitions of "appretiance" imply, when we deliberately seek out and notice those qualities that we hold in high estimation, our act of noticing and valuing actually amplifies those qualities and increases their value. Put simply, "What we dwell upon expands." Asking appreciatively focused questions heightens the possibility of seeing and creating more value in the object of inquiry.

To *inquire* means to search and discover. Inquiry is the act of exploration, a questioning with an agenda to see new possibilities. *AI always begins with a question—an honest desire to learn about something—at its premise.* It is not only about mobilizing human resources to change or to "buy in" to a strategy that has already been derived. It is about learning together so that the generative power of strength-based inquiry can propel innovation and change. AI is a constructive, generative, and capacity building mode of action-research in which inquiry, learning, *and* change are seen as a related, integral whole.

It is fruitful to focus attention on the world we want rather than focusing on eliminating what we don't want. This requires us to ask questions that *seek to locate what is preferred.* AI involves, at its root, the art and practice of crafting questions that support a system's capacity to apprehend, anticipate, and heighten positive potential. AI is a quest to discover the "positive core" of a system—the past, present, and future capacities to cooperate for the common good. The questions asked about a human system will lay the groundwork for the direction of the system's growth. As noted above, what we dwell upon expands. The pragmatic core of AI proposes that it is the questions that count most. Consider this vignette.

We recently worked with a pharmacist assistant in the Navy who is the last person the patient sees before leaving the clinic, having seen a physician and/or nurse and been given a prescription. This person's job was to dispense the filled prescription and make sure the patient was educated about how to take the medicine. As he related his story, his last instruction always came as a request, "Would you please call me in 48 hours and let me know how you are feeling?" By his account, the results were roughly 50/50. That is, half would call back and complain that they were not getting any better or that they felt worse. Half said they were doing OK or feeling much better.

Informed about AI, he decided to experiment with a new request, "Would you please call me in 48 hours and tell me how *well* you are doing?" With this simple, yet powerful, change in wording he reported astounding results after several weeks. The ratio of people reporting that they were feeling better and that the prescription was having a positive impact went up to 80/20.

AI offers a method that seeks to cultivate innovation and change while becoming unlocked from conventional assumptions regarding diagnosis and problem solving. AI selectively seeks to locate, highlight, and illuminate the life-giving properties of any given organization or human system. These kinds of efforts to discover and theorize about the life-giving properties of organizations—what is happening when they are operating at their best—is more likely than problem-solving to lead to innovation and capacity *building*.

In AI, one assumes that the positive exists and is only yet to be discovered. We begin any inquiry with the assumption there are already factors and forces in the system that give life, that support vitality, that lead to successful outcomes. This has implications for how we design questions that lead to discovery, a point we will explore later in this book. So when the word "inquiry" is placed after the word "appreciative," we emphasize a deliberate, committed, open ended search; a mutual interdependence and collaboration in seeking those life-giving forces that we most value. AI is, above all, a quest for learning (rather than for a solution to a problem). AI puts all the emphasis and value on the search for new, shared understandings of what has already caused the system to be at its best.

If we really valued the power of inquiry—the powerful and fateful potency of the questions we ask—we might not need the word "appreciate" at all. In our work with AI we have come to see time and time again that *we live into the world our questions create.*

**TRY THIS**

The next time you sit down with the family for dinner or sit with a friend over coffee, instead of saying, "How did your day go" or "How's it going," try this question: "What's the single best thing that happened to you today?" See if the conversation changes. See how you feel.

*There is no such thing as a neutral question.*

## Chapter 5

# Re-thinking Human Organization And Change

There are two clear benefits from using Appreciative Inquiry (AI) to build capacity through exploring and focusing attention on successes, strengths, and moments of greatest efficacy:

1.  Our inquiry is self-fulfilling: we see and create more of the world that we are seeking;
2.  Such inquiry is generative: it creates more hope and confidence in the human capacity to achieve something together, and thereby calls us to do so.

It is in this sense that we can see AI as a powerful form of capacity building. It helps to uncover, or reconnect with, past cooperative capacity. This inquiry fosters a collective desire to make additional, innovative efforts to cooperate in the future by helping to create shared, positive, and attractive images of a desired state. These future images are inspirations that call people to want to co-construct actions or initiatives so as to live together into the future they most want.

When living within an appreciative framework, human systems develop an expansive competence, an ability to see the nascent potential and radical possibilities that expand beyond the boundaries of problems as they might be presented in conventional terms. AI takes seriously the notion that how we live our life is a function of where we put our collective attention—that where we focus our collective attention leads to the choices we consider and act upon. By doing so, it provokes the question: What happens if we turn our attention to what is most valuable, life giving and vibrant in a human system?

Work using AI in all parts of the globe and in all levels of human systems (families, teams, schools, business units, global alliances) is consistently revealing and supporting fundamental *and provocative* notions about human organizations and change. There are six principles we have found most compelling and validated in our work with AI. They are described below. David Cooperrider originally framed the first five principles; the sixth is our addition.

### The Constructionist Principle: As We Talk, So We Make

The constructionist principle stems from the seminal work of social constructionists Ken Gergen[9] and Ted Sarbin.[10] Social constructionist thought proposes that we create the world that we call "real" through our words — our conversations, symbols, metaphors, and stories. Words are more than just utterances, rhetorical devices, or conduits containing information; they are formative in guiding how people construct the world, the resources that guide how people actually "have" experiences. In conversations together we create the organizational world that we then experience as normal and real. And we create the world through the words we have available to us. Would it be possible to perceive and treat someone as a "high achiever" if there were no such words to label his/her behavior? It is a term that might make sense within a Fortune 500 Company or amongst MBAs, but would be less useful, if even known, for members of a commune or a church gathering. Every vocabulary identifies and validates certain kinds of actions. Would it be possible to notice teamwork and cooperation if there were not an entire network of categories, metaphors, and stories that lend sense and meaning to some locally valued actions?

Words emerge within the context of interpersonal exchanges. Commitments are forged, relationships are formed, futures are negotiated, all based on the words deemed available and the topics that become the focus of conversation. This is what we mean when we say "words create worlds." For example, to refer to an organizational member as a "subordinate" is not a neutral act.[11] It triggers a whole family of terms and categories that guide action and deem some utterances appropriate and others not. That family of terms includes references to hierarchy, chain of command, superiors, controls, and so on. In this sense, a single word is never a single word, but rather a link to a worldview. Thus altering the everyday vocabulary in a social system has potentially powerful consequences.

In one organization, for example, a decision was made to refer to all employees as "associates." At first this seemed inconsequential, but soon the implications of this small change began to reverberate in increasingly radical ways enabling the adoption of participative decision-making and various forms of workplace democracy.[12] When language begins to change, whole new possibilities open up. Behind this is a powerful and subtle social dynamic.

The words we use guide what we notice, and indeed how we interpret, our experiences. Words are not neutral: they are always the product of human relationships. This shifts the way we think about language. The ways we talk, the words at our disposal, are tools that help us construct and live in the world. In the words of Wittgenstein, "The limits of my vocabulary are the limits of my world."[13] This implies that when we create new stories, new metaphors, and new language, we are changing the very fabric of the organization.

*We need to think of words as actions, as powerful tools that do things. This is an insight that great leaders seem to instinctively know. In fact, this might be the central responsibility—to define and redefine reality for organization members. In a recent interview, Admiral Vernon Clark, the then Chief of Naval Operations, put it this way: "Leaders get to paint the picture for others to walk into. And the words they use are very important."*

**The Poetic Principle: As We Choose Topics of Inquiry, So We Open New Horizons of Action**

The word "poetic" comes from the Greek "poesis" and means, "to make or create." AI celebrates this notion by suggesting that organizations are open-ended, evolving networks of possibilities open to an endless variety of perspectives. In short, organizations are human inventions, like poetry, that can be made and re-made, created and re-created. Creating or choosing topics of inquiry helps to create and promote organizational growth and development. The poetic principle means that we can choose to learn more about *any* topic within *any* organization. For instance, we can choose to notice or study the dynamics of stress, conflict, competition, or breakdowns—or we can choose to look into the dynamics of hope, cooperation, competence, or growth. Virtually any topic is fair game. It's important to notice that *the topic we study is a decisive act.* Like most decisions it is best to be thoughtful and purposeful when choosing. The poetic principle reminds us to be conscious of choosing where we want to put our attention because what we focus on will grow and expand.

A bold choice of topics for further study is a move that can be generative, can challenge assumptions, and can open up new possibilities for action. More specifically, choosing a positive, hopeful topic for further inquiry will dislodge old patterns, interrupt taken-for-granted assumptions, provoke wonderment, and lead to capacity building. Consider the following interaction reported by David Cooperrider. He is counseling a consultant to a Fortune 500 firm where the consultation has been directed at reducing sexual harassment lawsuits. The consultant is part of a widely recognized group of specialists on gender conflict and diversity issues. For the past two years the group has been trying to help their client reduce the complaints and lawsuits related to sexual harassment. By all accounts, they admit, the problem has continued to grow. So the following interaction occurs:[14]

D.C.          Before we get into our proposal, we have an im-
              portant question. What is it that you want to learn
              about and achieve with this whole intervention, and
              by when?

Consultant:   We want to dramatically cut the incidence of sexual
              harassment. We want to solve this huge problem,
              or at least make a significant dent in it.

D.C.          OK...But is that all?

Consultant:   You mean what do I really want to see? (Long
              pause...then she blurts out her response.) What we
              really want to see is the development of the new
              century organization—a model of high quality,
              cross-gender relationships in the workplace.

The new topic—a model of high quality cross-gender relationships—was used to invite volunteer male-female pairs to help the
company study and learn from the best examples of working relationships between men and women in their organization. Hundreds
stepped forward to participate. Learning of this experiment, another consulting firm (Marge Schiller & Associates) similarly transformed an identical problem into a generative topic at Avon-Mexico.
The resulting intervention changed the culture so dramatically that
Avon-Mexico was awarded the 1997 Catalyst Award for "Best Place
to Work in the Country for Women."

> *There is nothing about the organizational*
> *world itself that dictates what there is to be*
> *studied. The implication for practice is this:*
> *What we study—what we ask questions*
> *about—should be guided by the vision of the*
> *world we want to co-create.*

**The Principle of Simultaneity: As We Ask Questions, So We Become Transformed (and in turn, Transform What We Ask About)**

Inquiry is intervention. The seeds of change are planted with the very first questions we ask. The moment we begin to explore a topic, we already change the "targeted" situation. Simply put, the simultaneity principle suggests that inquiry and change are not separate undertakings. The questions we craft *guide* conversations, shape what people discover and pursue, and instill certain images/expectations of the future. Therefore if we ask organizational members about creative collaboration in the organization, we are setting the stage for the "respondent" to recall such moments, to create or maintain a discourse that tracks moments that lead to creative collaborations, the benefits of collaboration, and so on. And, as we said earlier about the power of words, stories tend to resonate with members of the organization. After leaving a conversation about creative collaboration, participants begin to notice new spaces and possibilities for better collaboration, recall other moments of successful collaboration, or begin to notice small, previously unnoticed gestures as invitations to collaborate. In short, questions of this kind seed networks of conversations and create environments that bring positive attention to desired categories and behaviors.

> *Since every question into a social topic begins a conversation that creates, maintains or transforms a way of being and doing, there is no such thing as a 'neutral' question.*

**The Anticipatory Principle: As We Anticipate, So We Create**

The anticipatory principle begins with what seems to be a counterintuitive hypothesis: if you want to change an existing human system, first change the *future*. More specifically, this principle suggests that perhaps the most potent vehicle for transforming human systems is our projection of a future image. But, you might ask, what does a future image have to do with present behavior? The collective image of the future, as projected in ongoing conversations and categories of discourse, guides what there is to notice in the present, and by doing so, structures action. The philosopher Martin Heidegger outlined how we are always creating and anticipating "forestructures."[15] We are always projecting ahead of ourselves a horizon of expectations that brings possible future pathways into the present. We anticipate the future; we project likely maps of that future; and then we proceed to live "as if" the future were already happening.

Futurist Elise Boulding understood the power of future imagery and warned that a world of technocratic problem solvers may be truncating our capacity to create positive images. She insisted that we need to cultivate "image literacy"—the capacity to form hopeful, anticipatory images of the future. In an age of incredible technological achievement, we may blindly begin to assume that every human challenge has a technological solution. When we face large challenges, we passively wait for some expert to provide a technological solution: The United Nations will fund a commission that will solve the problem of world hunger; the US Congress will establish a commission to investigate 9/11 and develop plans and policies to prevent such horror from ever occurring again; the US Pentagon's Ballistic Missile Defense Organization will protect us from ICBMs launched from other countries. The unintended consequence of such faith in technological advances is the surrender of our own imagination, our own collective ability to fashion a creative solution.

The capacity to create positive, anticipatory images of the future is a skill that we need to acknowledge and develop. The field of sports psychology has shown for some time that the formation of positive imagery is a potent tool. Studies of Olympic champions and the best professional athletes reveal that they learn and master the skill of imaging the perfect performance better than their competitors. Recovering or developing such "image literacy" involves multiple ways of knowing (not just cognitive, logical ways of knowing) as well as multiple, strengthening faculties—our intuition, our caring capacity, and our bonding instincts. Boulding fears that we are losing our image literacy, that capacity to "combine the materials of inner and outer experience worlds, drawn from all the senses to shape new patterns of 'reality.' Children do it all the time, but it is called daydreaming, and they are punished for it."[16]

> *Positive images of the future may be so powerful that they guide us at the cellular level. Studies of the placebo effect, for instance, have demonstrated that images of health and well-being might play an important part in actually releasing the bodily mechanisms necessary for healing and recovery.*

### The Positive Principle: As We Discover Moments of Hope, Joy, and Caring, So We Enjoy Generative Experiences

The positive principle holds that organizations are responsive to positive images and positive language. It is important not to shy away from the "positive" in this formula. In the world of day-to-day relationships, negotiations, and coordinated activity, it seems absurd to pretend that affect and emotion do not, or should not, play a role in how work proceeds. Humanistic psychology has outlined the power of positive regard and supportive affect in building or sustaining cooperative capacity. People and organizations are, indeed, *heliotropic*; that is, they tend to grow in the direction of the helio, or life source. To grow "toward the light" of a positive anticipatory image suggests that conversations embedded in hope, joy, inspiration, and other positive affect are *key* contributors (not by-products) to lasting change and enduring health. Building and sustaining momentum for change requires new combinations and networks of committed relationships. Committed relations only tend to flourish under conditions of hope, excitement, and caring.

Simply put, the more unconditionally positive the questions we ask, the more opportunities we build to create and sustain a generative discourse that is essential to building cooperative capacity.[17] Experience with AI change efforts suggests that people are deeply moved and committed when asked questions about those moments in their experience that were life-giving and hope-producing. Hopeful images of the future, when linked to actual experiences, are compelling and attractive, and when shared, they create social bonds that expand cooperation, deepen collaboration, and move us "toward the light."

*Hopeful imagery, embedded in discourse, attracts energy and mobilizes intention and action. Positive conversations* **lead** *to positive actions.*

### The Narrative Principle: As We Weave Stories, So We Create Lasting Bonds

As more and more reports, case studies, and stories of AI reach us,[18] it has become clear that the act of sharing stories about the best of the past initiates powerful interaction and relationships from which cooperation and desire to change ensues. This is a theme we will explore in the next chapter. The narrative principle celebrates the power of stories as a catalyst for change.[19] Often when organizational members share their peak experiences or moments of magnified meaning, the narratives take on the character of sacred stories that carry cultural meanings. By this we do not mean "sacred" in a strictly religious sense; rather, organization members tell one another stories that are deeply valued, durable, and persistent. These stories become powerful resources to draw upon when needed.

As children of all ages know, there is something magical about good stories. We learn things at deep levels through hearing and telling stories. We pay attention to good stories; they move us before we know why we are being moved; they impact us before we have time to put up defenses. They give shape to our hopes, wishes, and fears. Stories also remind us of our most important values. Stories—not lists and wall plaques—reveal deeply held values, turning points, and amazing acts that give texture to the culture. The stronger that culture is, the more enduring and successful the enterprise.[20]

Stories provide coherence. A coherent sense of movement and direction is central to a meaningful life. Without them, life is series of random, unconnected happenings. The past, present, and future are not separate unconnected stages, but rather beginnings, middles and endings—parts, in other words, of a *story in progress*. We rely upon stories to make our lives meaningful to our selves and to one another. Sharing stories also builds bonds. By engaging in stories, we connect with others and we learn.

**TRY THIS!**

Organizations and human systems are stories-in-progress. All the members are co-authoring particular stories every day. No human event in the system has meaning apart from a story. At the beginning of the next meeting you chair or attend, suggest that the first 10 minutes be the sharing of stories about the most positive experiences people have had since the last meeting. You will see amazing shifts in the way your team engages with the rest of the work agenda for the meeting.

## Chapter 6

# What Does The Practice
# Of AI Look Like?

In this chapter, we will discuss the practice of building cooperative capacity through Appreciative Inquiry (AI) in finer detail, and describe the phases and activities that organizations experience as they engage in AI. First we must emphasize that AI centers around *two basic questions*:

1. What in this particular setting has already made (your strategic topic/focus) possible?
2. What possibilities exist, expressed or latent, to do (strategic topic/focus) even better in the future?

It is the first question that makes AI unique and, as discussed earlier, fateful. You can insert *any* capacity building topic, opportunity, or issue into the parentheses. AI has helped organizations to study, and ultimately improve, "capacity building topics" ranging from optimal margins to extraordinary teamwork, from leadership at every level to exceptional arrival experiences, from creating innovative breakthroughs to providing an information power advantage, and from setting goals that change the world for children to business as an agent for world benefit. Remember from the previous discussion of the Poetic Principle, one can do an appreciative inquiry into any subject. The key is that it is strategically relevant and attractive to those invited into the inquiry.

The first question above is a departure from conventional thinking. The question suggests that the organization or system *already* contains significant cooperative capacity that has sustained its existence over time. Why invoke the past to change the future? Indeed, many would agree with GE's Jack Welch saying, "Yesterday is over; learn from it, but move on."[21] But it is the "learn from it" idea that we think has been almost ignored for the sake of "moving on." When the best and the brightest are convened to do strategic planning or visioning, they are usually invited to begin with the second question above. Encouraged to think "out of the box," they fill whiteboards with ideas for future scenarios that, at best, are logical, incremental extensions of the status quo. Most really bold ideas are self-censored because the history they are carrying in their memories is typically one of constraints, scarce resources, and previously nominated bold ideas that were shot down by someone else in the group. Whatever the reason, it is a limited view of history that guides the generation of ideas.

By asking the "best of the past" question first, we reconnect with those moments in history that reveal, upon guided inquiry, those processes, factors, and behaviors that enabled the system to do something extraordinary. We call these things the "positive core." And with this positive core freshly embedded in one's consciousness, the dreams and ideas about future possibilities (the second question) become bolder, broader, and more *un*common. So with these two basic questions, AI creates a shift in direction, away from the incremental drift of most strategic planning processes.

### The 4-Ds: Discovery, Dream, Design, and Destiny

The process of AI can be visualized as a cycle through four stages[22] or phases of activity: discovery, dream, design, and destiny as shown in Figure 2 below. While this diagram remains the most often used depiction of the AI process, it is important to remember that AI is a dynamic process and the "Ds" simply represent different, intentional sets of activities and conversations, all linked to an affirmative inquiry topic (see Chapter 7 for more on the "defining" of a topic). The linearity of this diagram should not be mistaken for a "forced march" agenda that one must follow.

Each of the "Ds" signify a focused, task-oriented, collaborative conversation that is essential to an appreciative inquiry, be it in a coaching dyad, a team, the merging of two departments, the entire organization, or an association of organizations/constituencies. AI is not just engaging in positive feedback, or just story-telling, or just imagining the future, or just thinking and talking about what is right or good. It is a disciplined choreography of conversation, reflection, analysis and imagination among various parties.

**Figure 2: The 4 D Process: From a Roadway Express Summit at their Akron Terminal**

As noted earlier, our most exciting work with AI recently has been with large groups, or "whole system" summits. Remembering that the 4-Ds could be applied to one other, or a group, or to groups of groups, we invite you in the rest of this chapter to consider these stages in the context of how they look in an AI Summit where large numbers of multi-stakeholders gather to address some strategic opportunity with the intent to increase their cooperative capacity to launch positive change initiatives on behalf of the *whole* system. The rest of this chapter will guide you through this process with examples showing what groups actually do and accomplish along the way. *One specific example we will draw upon is a large, multi-stakeholder group summit using AI at Roadway Express. At*

*various points, we will refer to Appendix 1 where we have included*
*the actual worksheets and task guidelines that participants used in*
*that setting.*

# Discovery

---

The Discovery phase centers on the inquiry into the Best of the
Past. This is where the "inquiry" dimension of Appreciative Inquiry is paramount; where the transformational learning journey
begins. Through an intentional protocol, questions are asked to
solicit stories and experiences of when an organizational factor was
at its very best, most effective, most prevalent, etc. Once positive
topics are chosen—such as Transformational Collaboration or
Empowering Leadership—stories of these high-point experiences
are shared and probed for underlying meaning or lessons. Both the
storyteller and listener(s) dig for underlying factors that "give life"
to the topic in question. Storytelling is essential in this initial activity. As described in Chapter 4 (see the Narrative Principle),
storytelling immediately gives everyone a voice in the process,
suspending evaluation and criticism while valuing something in
each and every response.

### Beginning Discovery
The process of discovery begins when participants interview each
other with appreciatively focused questions. Within this conversation, stories of strength are revealed that are often reminders of
accomplishments and experiences that were surprising and elevat-
ing—perhaps even life-giving. Further, the appreciative protocol
encourages each party to probe deeply into his other partner's stories in order to dig out the underlying causes or factors for success.
This is where the inquiry in AI is paramount. The listener is often
reminded to "mine for the gold in the other's story."

The pair's discoveries are then shared with other pairs in small groups to seek out the most common, life-giving factors that underlie the collection of stories. As this common ground of root causes of success emerges, the "positive core" or "DNA for success" is revealed. The outcome or product of this discovery work is the articulation of key strengths of the system (or team, division, or individual); capabilities that have already enabled it to empower members, further teamwork, optimize margins (or whatever topic the organization wants to learn more about).

For example, at Roadway Express's[23] Akron terminal (referred to as 211) there was a recurring problem (as the corporate leadership phrased it) with "throughput:" the time it takes for incoming freight to be unloaded, sorted, reloaded, and out of the terminal. In a trucking business with small margins, fifteen minutes of unnecessary time in the terminal equates to lost revenue per shipment. Corporate management had designated "throughput" as the topic for this Roadway site to address. A local team of 13 people, including terminal managers, supervisors, union (Teamster) stewards, a clerk, drivers, dock workers, a sales representative, and a divisional executive, met to discuss the topic in order to begin an AI learning process. It was clear from the start that if management wished to convene any group of employees to look at "throughput" they would be met with skepticism and resistance for trying another "speed up tactic." So the group shared stories of times when the throughput had been at its best and times when they individually had done something to hasten freight through the site. They worked hard for a half-day and finally were asked; "What purpose statement or topic for this AI process would most excite your fellow workers/managers, most stimulate their curiosity and result in a future you really wish for?" From "throughput" they agreed on a new Topic Statement:

Winning with Employee Driven Throughput:
Crushing non-union competition by delivering unsurpassed speed and leveraging employee pride and involvement.

## Taking It to the Whole System

With this topic, the Discovery began by bringing together over 180 people for three days in a hotel ballroom (See Appendix 1: pp. 107-111), representing the union, management, drivers, dock workers, forklift operators, clerks, supervisors, salespersons, customer representatives and customers. They were broken up into mixed pairs so that drivers interviewed dock workers, forklift operators interviewed salespersons, and so on. They were asked to interview each other using the following questions: (See Appendix 1: pp. 112-114 for interview protocol)

### Winning with Employee Driven Throughput

Throughput represents how quickly we can process the freight through our facility. We win the battle for the 1 & 2 day market when we accelerate the processing of freight from pick-up, through the 211 gate, across the dock, and down the road. System *speed*...that's our need. If we can achieve maximum throughput, we will crush the non-union regional carriers and we will dominate the market.

**Question 1:** Think back to a time at work that you recall as a "highpoint"...an experience or moment you remember as having left you with an <u>intense sense of pride, excitement, or involvement</u> in having been a part of something that was meaningful...a time that you truly felt you had contributed to the betterment of a fellow employee(s), the customer, or the organization.

Describe that experience; what was going on, who was involved, what made it so memorable?

**Question 2:** Tell me about a time when you thought throughput (speed) was at its best at 211, or when you were involved in moving a shipment quickly through facility to final destination in order to meet a customer requirement.

Tell the story of what was going on—who was involved and what happened.

What did you do? What did you value most about your involvement in that story?

What do you value most about the contribution of others in that story?

**Surfacing the Stories**

These questions surfaced many positive stories.[24] They helped set the stage for participants to Dream, or imagine, what the organization might look like if there were more examples like the ones shared during the interviews: stories of dockworkers organizing without supervision to handle breakdowns or sudden crises; stories of drivers educating and helping customers to have freight ready earlier and easier to load; stories of supervisors relating to union members in ways that created a "team feeling" in the terminal; stories of people going beyond their job descriptions to help out because it was the "right thing to do;" and stories of senior union members teaching and helping younger members to work more productively. (See Appendix 1: pp. 115-116)

To summarize, the Discovery phase invites participants to reflect on the "best of the past" with respect to some chosen, strategic topic and then to rigorously examine those stories of the past for underlying factors, forces and conditions that helped make them happen. Together, these "life-giving" factors comprise the "positive core" or strength-base for further cooperative capacity building.

# Dream

When the best of "what is" has been discovered, conversation naturally turns to imagining new possibilities. Capacity building through visioning a preferred future involves "passionate thinking" about a positive image of a desired future state. Keeping in mind the key strengths (from the Discovery work described above) already present in the system, the Dream stage extends what is currently possible to "imagining all that could be;" generating images of the ideal state that we really wish for. Again, the questions or conversation starters here are fateful. Rather than asking, "What should we be doing in the future?" or even "What do you most desire for a future here?" a story or narrative is solicited. A typical vision or dream question would be to ask a participant to imagine awakening from a long sleep and going to work and discovering that a miracle has occurred—everything is just as you always wished for. The participant is invited to describe what she/he sees, what is going on, with whom, and so on, as if they are in that future, now. The purpose is to elicit images and stories first—openings for others to supplement or complement—not lists or opinions. Participants are often encouraged to present their ideal future images using skits, songs, or poetry in order not to fall into more customary meeting norms of sharing lists, phrases, and opinions that invite evaluation or criticism.

For example, at Roadway 211 (the example above) participants were asked to imagine an ideal future state from this question[25]:

> **Question:** <u>Tomorrow's reality</u>. Imagine that you have awakened from a deep sleep and 3 years have passed. Roadway dominates the non-union regional carriers in the marketplace! Wall Street is buzzing over the dramatic success Roadway has had in the regional markets! Articles in *Transport Topics* describe how Roadway—by tapping into the pride and involvement of its employees—has leveraged a dramatic improvement in *speed* at the 211 complex! This muscular, yet agile system has catapulted Roadway Akron to the forefront in reducing costs while establishing unparalleled levels of customer service and employee satisfaction. For customers, it's now *imperative* that they do their 1 & 2 day regional business with 211/Akron! For employees, 211 is a place that they would rather work than any other place!
>
> What happened to allow for this kind of success?

What part did you play in this success?

What 3 wishes do you have to help Akron Roadway reach and sustain this success?

## Selecting the Common Elements

At the Roadway Summit, these questions triggered a variety of creative images and stories. After sharing these images and wishes, groups selected the most common elements among their varied images of the preferred future. (See Appendix 1: pp. 117-118) They then created innovative ways to portray some aspect of their shared vision of the ideal future. One group created a skit showing one shift passing out of the main gate and "high fiving" (clapping hands with) the new shift entering. Another group showed a mock interview with a new customer to see if they aligned with Roadway's values and deserved to become a "preferred" customer. There was a skit in which a driver actually creates new business by helping a customer at their docking bay and another portrayed a union member using an electronic kiosk to access benefits and scheduling information. One presentation showed a group of dock workers running their own stand-up meeting in the early morning at the beginning of their shift to communicate the priorities for the day.

The outcome or product of the Dream phase is the articulation of the most common elements of the preferred future. The Dream phase often includes a visual mapping of opportunities or change ideas based upon the ideal images that people hear and see in the presentations of creative skits and discussions of the dream question. (See Appendix 1: p. 118)

In this instance at Roadway, the group of around 180 participants at tables of eight each generated 67 change ideas to help move toward the ideal images and wishes they had shared and portrayed to each other. This was a process of handing a microphone around to each group who, in turn, read out one of their top three ideas/opportunities for change. These were recorded on a large white board or flip chart as they were called out (written as spokes emanating from a circle in the center of the board with the Affirmative

Topic written in it). After two or three rounds through all the tables, everyone's ideas were up and they were invited to use "sticky dots" to vote on the three ideas or opportunities they found most attractive and important to pursue. The resulting "clusters" of ideas that received the most votes are described below:

Roadway Express Opportunity Map Summary

- Ready Freight Earlier (coordination between drivers and dock operation to better anticipate local freight arrivals and turnaround)
- All Stakeholders Engaged: (Communications more timely information at beginning of shifts to identify priorities, problems from prior shift, staffing concerns, etc.)
- Bridging the Gap: Bidding Process (periodic process for union members to "bid" for preferred job roles and shifts)
- Bridging the Gap: Attendance (minimizing last-minute or unexcused absences)
- Bridging the Gap: Positive Pride (supervisor-subordinate relations to engender pride and respect)
- Educating and Leveraging Employee Experience (mentoring by senior union members to more junior members to create more responsibility for total organization success and therefore more healthy and sustainable pensions)
- Measurement, Technology, Procedures and Equipment (use of technology to enhance speed and throughput)

In summary, the Dream phase invites participants to use the knowledge and excitement about possibilities gained from the Discovery to imagine what could be in an ideal future. The Discovery interviews *generate* a desire to articulate bolder possibilities because confidence in the whole system's capacity to be effective has been elevated. The sharing of the ideal images is often the most fun-filled, joyous, and energizing part of the 4-D process. Participants are frequently surprised at at the similar themes represented in their visions. Finally, by brainstorming all the possible actions, changes, or opportunities that are reflected in the shared dreams, participants are ready to launch into more practical Design, or action-planning.

# Design

In the Dream phase, people imagine new dimensions, outcomes, and results. The Design phase addresses the question: What kind of organizational forms, policies, and structures will enable the cooperative capacity necessary to make these imaginative outcomes and highest wishes become a reality? The Design phase, it can be said, is aligned with concepts from the field of architecture. Anyone who has been involved in a construction project knows about the importance of design and anyone who has worked with a good architect knows the excitement that ensues when the design brings dreams to life. Designing involves creating the foundations upon which guiding structures are built. Just as architects design the structures that become the containers and boundaries that facilitate sets of activities, so in the design phase of a change project, the core structural elements—leadership, reward systems, and so on—generate principles and propositions that become the foundation that supports projects and activities.

## Transformative Action

The Design phase begins the transformation from stories, dreams, ideas, and feelings to actions and projects. Here, participants in an Appreciative Inquiry choose which ideas and images from the Dream stage are most attractive to them, so compelling that they want to *personally* work to make them a reality. By this stage of the 4-D process, participants tend to see the organizational system as a synthetic whole. Because members are interacting with a diverse group, they don't just speak out of their own narrow self-interest. As more and more common threads and factors are discovered through Discovery and Dream work, the dialogue begins to take the entire system into account. In this Design phase, participants dialogue about the preferred shape of the organization and what crucial structural elements might be needed to support their preferred future or shared list of opportunities.

## Two Approaches to Design

We have used two approaches to do the Design work. The first centers on this question: how do elements in the formal organization need to be created or transformed in order to support our ideals and allow our shared dream to flourish? Here we encourage members to consider the structural mechanisms that guide and give shape to action. Sometimes we use organizational models such as the McKinsey 7 S model—how would we design or shape superordinate goals, systems, strategies, structures, styles of management, staffing, etc. to create the future we want? Other areas for consideration may emerge from the positive core that came out of the Discovery phase: education and training, leadership style, culture, work processes and job design, information systems, and so on.

Example One: The United States Environmental Protection Agency's Division of Research used the AI process to engage nearly 400 of its research staff in designing their future. The design areas around which people were invited to engage were as follows:

| | |
|---|---|
| Education and Training | Reward and Recognition Practices |
| Leadership Style and Culture | Decision Making Procedures |
| Staff/People/Relationships | Beliefs about People |
| Beliefs about Power and Authority | Communications |
| Work Processes & Job Design | Recruiting Practices |
| Career Structures & Incentives | Balance of Personal / Professional Life |
| Organizational Structures Information | Systems and Technology |
| Stakeholder Relationships | Planning Methods |
| Information Systems | |

Sub-groups of participants are given one of the above areas to develop more specific aspirations. They are asked to design principles or "provocative propositions" to guide how this part of the organization could be structured, managed, or designed in order to best align with the shared themes from the Dream work.

A second approach to the Design Phase is to ask participants to generate possible change initiatives, opportunities, or actionable ideas directly from the visions and imagery expressed in the Dream phase: What kinds of projects, initiatives or changes will most support our shared vision of the ideal future?

Example Two: This example is taken from the Roadway Express Opportunity Map Summary described above (in Dream section). Recall that the 180 participants in the AI session generated 67 different ideas for changes that would help them reach the future images they had revealed in the Dream Stage. They were then asked to take a stand and vote for the change ideas that each person felt were the most important next steps for the organization. Each person had three sticky dots to use to "vote" by placing them next to the change idea/opportunity that he or she most wanted to work on to make a reality. Based on the dot voting, seven top priority areas were determined. Groups then self-formed around the priority area they most wanted to help make happen. They "vote with their feet" and go to the opportunity or change idea they most want to work on. It is important to note that these new groupings are still mixed with the various stakeholder voices in attendance (e.g. management, union, sales, office personnel, customers). Each newly formed group is given a chance to request more of a particular stakeholder input before they set off to design their action plans.

### Provocative Propositions (or Aspiration Statements)
With either approach, the main work at this stage is prioritizing areas for change and developing "Provocative Propositions" or "Aspiration Statements" that describe some aspect of the desired organization as it "should be." *Provocative propositions are bold statements that stretch and challenge; they provoke the imagination to consider the positive core of the organization as already alive and vibrant.* These statements are exciting. They articulate the highest hopes and represent foundational beliefs (as in the Declaration of Independence: "We hold these truths to be self evident..."), and are written in the present tense, as if they are already happening. (See Appendix 1: pp. 118-119) These statements or propositions are vital in that they serve as guides, even motivating

tenets, for expanding the system's current cooperative capacity to new heights in order to achieve what is now collectively desired.

**Examples of Provocative Propositions**
The first example comes from the Roadway Express case we have been following. One self-selected team that chose to work on the "Freight Ready Earlier" change idea created the following Aspiration Statement:

> Roadway Express is the #1 transportation provider in the world due to our unsurpassed throughput service. "Team-sell" is contagious. Each employee is a stakeholder engaged in celebrating the success of the company. Customers are honored to have 211 [local site name] employees handle their business. All customer contact work groups are key components in our success. They are recognized as the best-trained, most highly motivated sales force in the universe.
> *NO COMPETITOR IS SAFE!*

In another example from the US Navy, a self-selected group of multi-stakeholders created the following example of a provocative proposition during an AI session devoted to supporting the growth and development of "leaders at every level."

> Navy Learning and Development:
> Education and training are the foundation of the empowered culture of excellence in the Navy. We foster leadership that encourages, challenges, and supports all members of the organization to engage in ongoing learning, both personal and professional. The Navy provides life long training and education opportunities that support a sense of purpose, direction, and continual growth. This, in turn, nurtures the strength and confidence people need to achieve their full personal and professional potential.

Conversations in this phase are constructed so that participants can seek and discover consensus, culminating in a statement such as:

"Yes, this is a specific ideal or project outcome that we value and should aspire to." Individual will—based upon a positive, anticipatory image or aspiration—transforms to a collective commitment.

Design in this sense is different from the way we think of decision-making. Traditionally we think of decisions as rational and "realistic" in the sense that they address the "way things are." The design attitude here is a more expansive approach in that it invites participants to think about creating the space and structures that allow the emergence of novel and generative action.

The actions being imagined and then planned at this stage and in the Destiny phase (below) are self-organized—the group takes on the responsibility and task of organizing for action. These self-selected, multi-functional, and multi-stakeholder groups are taking ownership for their work; their conversations are setting change in motion because they are discovering and choosing together what *they* will do beyond this meeting to make their provocative proposition become their reality.

In summary, we have increasingly found that the Design phase is one of the most potent in creating long-term differences in organizational futures. In this phase we have seen bold proposals to revamp career structures, revise the way rewards are allocated, create new forums for inclusive decision making, create new policies and strategies that open up new markets, launch new ventures, generate new revenues, eliminate barriers to innovation, open the "books" to every member so that they can act like owners, and redesign supply chains to speed product delivery. In this kind of designing (and in the Destiny phase that follows), participants are actually bringing a new organizational world into being—now—as opposed to planning for it in the abstract, or discussing how others will do it later on. Increased cooperative capacity is being enacted for all to witness.

## Destiny

---

The aim of the Destiny phase is to ensure that the shared dreams can be realized through the "blueprint" of desired actions/outcomes. To do this, participants in AI do specific action planning, scenario building, and role allocation for the necessary next steps. They also consider how they will expand the involvement in their change initiatives to others who may not be present but who are nonetheless vested in, or have expertise related to, the topic or change to be undertaken. The groups that generated the Aspiration Statements or Provocative Propositions in the Design phase present their implementation plans using a common template: (See Appendix 1: pp. 120-121)

Example: In the Roadway Express case we have been following, some of the action plans produced and initiated included:

- Supervisors and dock workers working together to experiment with short information exchanges at start of each shift that involve more union members initiating and leading discussions. (This has since catalyzed a major re-structuring of the dock workers into self-managed "zone teams" where supervisors are serving in new roles as mentors and coaches.)
- Local pick-up and delivery (P&D) drivers organizing and being equipped to generate new, short notice business from customers they see most often, becoming part of the customer sales representative team. (Now, these drivers have the title of Sales Associates, not P&D drivers.)
- Development and piloting of an electronic kiosk in the dock area for employees to get benefits/scheduling/announcement information.
- Pilot mentoring program involving senior union members coaching new/junior members to reduce absenteeism.

- Cross-functional team to reduce/reframe metrics and create training for the key metrics that monitor throughput.
- Union-management team to redesign process to deal with last minute or unannounced absences and warnings.

In addition to these specific, cooperative initiatives, there was capacity building at the organizational level that is worthy of note. One example began with the expressed wish or dream from drivers for air-conditioned cabs and the freedom to wear shorts in hot weather, which was prohibited by corporate policy. In the past, this request would not have been entertained. Management would have quickly said "no" to both and given cost and customer relations as the reasons, while silently feeling that this was another example of employee selfishness and lack of concern for company well-being. The remarkable conversation that ensued in this AI process went an entirely different way. One manager asked, "If air-conditioning would enhance employee-driven throughput, then how can we work together to generate higher margins so that there could be capital to invest in better cabs?" They also agreed, on the spot, to change the corporate policy regarding shorts. After a similar issue arose in one other AI process at another Roadway Terminal site, the organization recognized the need to have everyone understand how margins are created; how each job contributes to revenue and cost so that everyone can clearly see how an unexcused absence, for instance, incurs additional cost and negatively impacts margins, pensions, and customer service. They have since instituted education and training on these financial business factors for every member of the company.

In this specific case, the Roadway 211 terminal site committed to a follow-up meeting in six months that included half of the members of each of the action teams and an equal number of employees from all the different functional areas who were unable (or at that time unwilling) to participate in the initial AI process. By the time of the follow-up meeting, the following results had already been achieved:

**6 Month Outcomes from Roadway Express AI Summit:**
- Average throughput improved 47% to 64%
- Average transit speed reduced 2.3 days to 2.1 days
- Average production efficiency increased 59% to 64%
- Percent freight dispatched by 0500 increased 16% to 27%
- Greatly reduced need for formal grievance mechanisms

## Increased Momentum for Learning

In the Destiny phase, the organizational changes that multiple stake-holders generate come from a more spontaneous, self-organized movement than a pre-ordained plan, or a Gant Chart, or a neatly packaged or engineered flow-chart. The sense of momentum is apparent to all those involved and attention appropriately shifts to how this energy and focus will be sustained as participants return to the 'normal' workplace. One key to sustaining this learning 'movement' is to focus on the question, "how are we going to become a more appreciative learning culture?" [26]

Specific conversations are held to address how generative learning can be continued, accelerated, or expanded in the rest of the system. Typically these groups create plans to continue together and consider how to engage others. They often create a steering group and a dedicated website to monitor progress. The Destiny change initiatives typically require a virtual, community knowledge space for continuous exchange, reporting, monitoring, and further inquiry. At Roadway Express, for example, where they have conducted over 60 summits like the one we have described in this chapter, they recently held a virtual conference over their intranet with over 2000 participants from inside the company to share best practice ideas and changes that have come out of AI at various sites throughout North America. One new, company-wide initiative arising from that conference produced over $13 million in additional reported cost savings for 2004. An internal audit of this initiative revealed that those sites which had conducted one or more AI interventions like the one described here were able to achieve nearly *seven times the cost savings* of those sites who had not yet conducted any AI activities.

---

### The AI 4-D Cycle and Capacity Building
### at Roadway Express

During the past four years, Roadway Express (now Yellow-Roadway) has conducted over 60 AI interventions involving more than 10,000 of their employees. During this period the organization has improved its performance and the union-management culture has transformed to a real partnership, as indicated by the following:

- Recently featured in *Fast Company*
- From 300 to Zero grievances at one site
- Powerful product innovations
- Stock price more than doubled *during* recession years
- New culture of leadership and supervision: Developing/mentoring leaders at every level
- Powerful learning partnerships with Alcoa, Boeing, Cisco, Harley-Davidson, US Navy
- All employees educated and informed about how each job impacts margins and quality of service

---

## Summary

In this chapter we describe in detail the four phases that typically guide the process of Appreciative Inquiry—from Discovery that surfaces the core factors for success, to Dream that reveals the most shared images of a preferred future state, to Design where participants self-organize into cross-functional teams to create specific, actionable change targets or aspirations, to Destiny where these same groups self-organize and commit to actions, pilots, and projects that will move the organization towards realization of their preferred future. It is important to note again that throughout this 4-D cycle, or process, cooperative capacity is being built in two ways. The most obvious is that the outcomes from the process—the self-organized teams and the change projects they initiate—are all focused on system-wide change or improvement related to a strategic topic (Employee Driven Throughput, for example). These initiatives are devoted to changes that the participants believe will help them fulfill their shared vision of what they can achieve.

The power of the AI approach is embedded in the observation that *cooperative capacity is being built during the process.* Hundreds of stakeholders in a system are working together, discovering common history, preferred futures, and then co-authoring new aspirations and plans they publicly commit to making happen. Their confidence in each others' commitment and competence to deliver on their promises increases as the process goes on. Their willingness and capacity to cooperate is visibly greater than when they walked into the room to begin the 4-D process. They leave the process with plans and commitments to cooperate even more with each other and with those not yet able to be included in the changes that have been launched.

**FOCUS BOX**

The AI 4-D process of Discovery, Dream, Design. and Destiny provides a choreography of multi-stakeholder inquiry and dialogue that results in expanded abilities, desires, and commitments to cooperate for a common good. This 4-D process begins with co-inquiry into the best of the past in order to discover the positive core of the human system. This renewed connection to the system's greatest strengths enables members to dream boldly and confidently about a preferred future. With shared ideals in mind and the system's strengths at hand, members can then design initiatives, changes, and structures to move toward their shared vision of a preferred future. This co-construction of new cooperative ventures launches a new journey of learning, improvising, and appreciation that can re-generate itself. The building and expansion of cooperative capacity is limitless.

**Chapter 7**

# Getting Started: Choosing
# The Affirmative Topic

Now that the reader has some images of what the AI process is like—and what it can do—from Chapter 6, we turn our attention to how it begins. At the center of the "4-D" cycle described in the previous section is what we refer to as the Affirmative Topic. This is the domain or area for the inquiry; the focus of organizational learning. It represents the arena in which participants are invited to discover factors that are already helping us be at our best with this topic (e.g. teamwork, high margins, innovation, customer delight). The Affirmative Topic that builds cooperative capacity gives direction *and* signals possibility. Just as with the fateful question discussed in Chapter 4, the topic choice is a critical act. What we initially choose to work on and learn about predetermines the results we will, and will not, achieve. Cutting costs, while appropriate, will seldom lead to innovation. Investigating low morale will not reveal the secrets to high enthusiasm. Running focus groups to discover what causes customer dissatisfaction will not help us forge customer delight. Similarly, decades of research on "job satisfaction" and its relationship to productivity did not reveal the potential and power of "high enthusiasm" at work. Other examples might include studying employee longevity instead of turnover, or learning about the factors that cause abundance instead of poverty.

Thus, *AI begins with (re)framing* the situation or current state in such a way as to attract interest and generate hope or positive anticipation. *The effort here is to intentionally word the focus of the inquiry in such a way that it most captures what people are really curious about, what they really want to see as a desired outcome of working together.* Because of our tendency to rely upon deficit discourse (see Chapter 3), this is often a re-framing exercise. We are trained to identify problems and often forget that chasing the solution may just create another problem for someone else, or not get us much further toward what we really wish for. Yes, we all want problems to go away, but *toward what purpose*? What is the desired future on the other side of that problem? What is it we most wish for at the end of the day?

When this last question was posed to the executive leadership at British Airways, their ability to resolve a bothersome financial difficulty was transformed. They had been working for several years to "reduce lost and damaged baggage claim settlements" which were still increasing. The best industry consultants' recommendations had not righted the situation. So the new questioning began, "why do you want fewer claim settlements? What is it you really want to create?" As this line of inquiry progressed, the conversation shifted to what ideal state they were seeking. At one point, the group considered what kind of experiences would delight customers when they arrive at their destinations. Eventually they decided to inquire into "exceptional arrival experiences" of customers. Using the 4-Ds, they began an Appreciative Inquiry that eventually lead to innovative initiatives that increased customer service and finally reversed the lost and damaged baggage trend.[27]

Here are some examples of Affirmative Topics from our work and from the work of our colleagues that different organizations have created:

| | Original "Problem" | Affirmative Topic |
|---|---|---|
| Roadway Express | Improve Throughput | Winning with Employee-Driven Throughput: Crushing Non-union Competition by Delivering Unsurpassed Speed and Leveraging Employee Pride and Involvement. |
| US Navy | Increase Retention | Bold and Enlightened Naval Leaders at Every Level: *Forging an Empowered Culture of Excellence* |
| US Navy | Improve Image of IP Professionals | The Information Power Advantage *"Charting a Revolutionary Course"* <br>• Forge Information Dominance <br>• Lead the Evolution of the Warfighter <br>• Open Portals through Innovation |

| US Environmental Protection Agency | Improve Research Output | Working Together to Ensure the Earth's Vitality |
|---|---|---|
| Cleveland Clinic Foundation | Reporting Diagnostic Mistakes | Culture of Safety for All |
| World Vision | Translating Our Vision into a Strategic Plan | Setting the Goals that Change the World with Children |

Starting with an *intentional* topic choice is crucial because all human systems move in the direction of what they most deeply and persistently talk and ask questions about (see our discussion of the Constructionist Principle in Chapter 5). Like the 4-Ds, this is also a collaborative process. Often a design team or sub-group representing many of the stakeholder voices will work intensively to find a topic that will generate interest and enthusiasm among the potential invitees. Sometimes we find that people tend to want to rush through this work, or simply stay with the problem/opportunity-as-given. Indeed, they are mostly attracted by the image of getting a lot of their people together to work cooperatively on some strategic topic and to leave feeling more unified and involved. This is the moment we need to stop and remember that the key dynamic operating here is the *inquiry*. AI is not only about getting together and being positive with each other. The work done to find the generative, affirmative topic that people really want to understand better in order to imagine and realize more future possibilities is essential to this capacity building process.

We also continuously encounter the question, are there situations where AI would not work; where things are so bad or demoralized, or dysfunctional, that no one will wish to be positive? Our response is that we have not found any yet. No matter how bleak, hopeless, conflict-ridden, or problematic, the current situation appears to be, transformational, generative, and hopeful topics are possible in *any* situation and will lead to more and deeper positive change (see the Poetic Principle in Chapter 5). As we often remind people about to conduct an appreciative inquiry and who are wondering about people who want to discuss what is wrong, the loudest, most negatively worded and emotionally charged complaint is *also* the expression of an unmet wish. Lastly, while this kind of reframing is a learned skill, there is no "best answer" or "best topic."

**FOCUS BOX**

AI typically begins with a re-framing of a problem or issue of concern into an opportunity that is specifically worded in affirmative language that invites people to imagine a desirable possibility. The re-worded topic represents the group's answer to the basic question, "At the end of this, what is it we are really after?" It is not what you want to fix, but rather, what you want to build or create. That is why it ends up building capacity. You will know when you have your Affirmative Topic by the way people engage with it. Their interest and excitement for working on it will be high. They will be smiling.

**Chapter 8**

# Building Capacity For Teamwork: The Medic Inn Story

Here we present one of the earliest experiments with Appreciative Inquiry and one that clearly demonstrates the capacity building effect of using the approach outlined in the preceding Chapters.[28] While in Chapter 6 we described what an AI process might look like in a large, multi-stakeholder setting with hundreds participating, here we tell the story of a small management team responsible for running a hotel as part of a large health care institution. Whether applied in a group or in a large representation of the total system, AI is *generative*, by definition. It focuses on deeper understanding of current capacity to cooperate in order to imagine and develop more capacity to cooperate in the future. This is at the heart of the Medic Inn story.

Park Plaza was a flea-bitten, one-star hotel that was taken over by a new ownership group and challenged to transform itself. The mandate from the new owners to the managers of this low-cost, high turnover, poorly managed hotel was daunting: a rapid turn-around in service from a one-star to a four-star rating. The new owners immediately invested $15 million to transform the physical setting with marble floors, exotic furniture, new rooms, and the like. But because nothing was done on the human side, a year later it seemed to many that other than physical upgrades to the property, not much had really changed. We were asked to do action research that would engage everyone in the collaborative diagnosis and creation of an action plan that would help the hotel realize four-star status. In the meantime, employees were fearful of failure and firings; there was always the possibility of wholesale house-cleaning in any takeover of this kind.

While the story is very involved, there was one moment that created a powerful learning. We proposed in the organization assessment phase that we let go of all diagnostic, problem-oriented analysis—literally put a moratorium on all deficit analysis of low morale, turf issues, gaps in communications, mistrust, and bureaucratic breakdowns. We said that the deficit-based assumptions would make their organizational change come to a slow crawl if we continued to treat and define the system as "a problem-to-be-solved." We asked what would happen instead, if we engaged everyone in an inquiry with an alternative metaphor; that "organizations are centers of infinite relational capacity, alive with infinite imagination and open, indeterminate, and ultimately, in terms of the future, *mysteries*." The general manager objected, arguing for a problem solving approach and almost laughed when this was suggested. Two of his presenting "issues," for example, were horrendous guest responsiveness and a culture of not caring. So we proposed a *both/ and* scenario, in essence, an action-research experiment.

**A Tale of Two Inquiries**
We decided to divide the top group of 30 managers into two sub groups. One set of managers would be asked to do an organizational diagnosis. In one workshop the participants were given classic problem analytic models and problem-finding questions: *What are the largest barriers to your work? What are the causes of breakdowns in guest responsiveness?*

The second group had a workshop on AI. They were asked to "try on" the *half-full assumption*. We suggested that the capacity for caring was in fact present in the system and there were moments of exemplary guest responsiveness where employees far exceeded their job descriptions, going the extra mile, serving with passion. This was one of the core questions they used in interviews:

> *Revolutionary Guest Caring: The mark of our hotel when we have been really good, beyond even our most common best, has been those times we have responded to and exceeded our guest's expectations. Our assumption is that you too have been part of those times—perhaps at least once or many times. We want to know your story and then your vision of our future.*

*A. Can you share with me the story of when you were part of a successful, even revolutionary, moment of guest responsiveness — a time where you and others met and exceeded needs on both sides? Describe the situation in detail. What made it feel radically different? Who was involved? How did you interact differently, what were the outcomes and benefits you experienced?*

*B. Now with that story told, let's assume that tonight, after work, you fall asleep and do not wake up for ten years. But while asleep a miracle happened and our entire hotel, as an organization, became, during that decade, the kind of organization you would most like to see. Many positive changes have happened. So now you wake up, it is ten years later, and you come to this place. What do you see happening now that is different, new, better?*

When the two workshops were complete, it was time to ask the groups to do their separate interviews with different people in the hotel. No mention was made, however, about how the two groups differed. The different questions were *not* shared. Each separate group would do 30 interviews and prepare a report of their findings. They would come together in two weeks, for the first time, to share their organizational assessments.

So far, so good. That is, until the day of the report-outs when something rather amazing took place. The first group that volunteered to share their findings was the appreciative group. Each member was visibly excited and had a role in the presentation. Their energy was infectious. For one thing, they discovered that every employee they talked to wanted to participate in building a four-star vision and that there was one story after another of exceptional moments of guest responsiveness. In addition, the images of the future were compelling and inspired. The group shared inspiring quotes from the people they interviewed. The other group—the problem-finders—sat motionless. Then they made a forceful, almost accusatory query: "*Where did you find all this; certainly not here at this hotel with all its breakdowns? We did not hear anything like what you are saying? Why are you fabricating?*"

Now the tables turned. We said, "Hold on, let's give the other group a chance to report." So the second group presented (one person presented, the others sat back) a listing of about fifty serious problems, including negative supervision and inter-departmental frictions, followed by statistics on rock-bottom customer satisfaction. The scenario they painted of the future was dismal. It was loaded with a vocabulary of threat. Some people felt that all low performing personnel needed to be terminated; there were anonymous quotes that said the place should be closed down. The appreciative group questioned the authenticity of the data, asserting, "These are not the things we heard in the interviews." Both groups were now confused.

We then asked everyone to exchange interview guides and to pay close attention to the questions. It set the stage for one of the best conversations about the social construction of reality we have ever had: language and reality; the impact of analysis on our feelings of motivation and fear; the impact of human inquiry on the development of relationships; the idea of culture and narrative; notions of reflexivity and the "enlightenment" effect of inquiry; the relationship between inquiry and change.

Our pragmatic question for the general manager of the hotel was this: in relation to helping propel good change, which data set do you think would honestly bring people together to create the future you want? The story ends dramatically. The hotel embarked on a four-year process of AI and a doctoral dissertation by Frank Barrett traced the whole system transformation and showed how language *precedes* changes in structures, systems, policies, and even awareness.[29] A short time later the hotel received the coveted four-star status, without layoffs. We felt honored when an article we wrote on this case received Best Paper of the Year Award at the National Academy of Management.[30]

## AI and its Generative Capacity

A few implications from this experience deserve more comment. The first is the proposition that we *live in the world our questions create*. The questions we ask structure what we find; what we find becomes the basis for our conversation and dialogue; and this all becomes the ground from which we imagine, make sense of, narrate, theorize, speculate on, and construct our future together. Questions do more than gather information—they intervene. They are anything but neutral. Inquiry focuses attention and directs energy; it provides a container delimiting or expanding what is there to see; it affects rapport and relationships. It sets agendas for what is deemed important. When mindfully crafted to tap into generative potential, questions can trigger imaginative possibilities.

Consider the different approaches taken by two hypothetical supervisors. One supervisor begins the weekly meeting with: Why do we still have these problems? Why do you blow it so often? What barriers do you think we will face? Another asks: OK. group, let's start: What possibilities exist that we haven't yet thought about? What's the smallest change that could have the biggest benefit? Is there a new, more promising way to think about this?

The omnipresence of questions, and their inherent potential to evoke whole new worlds of possibilities, suggests a second insight that is even more central to AI. What we have found, in our own lives, is that *we too move—emotionally, theoretically, relationally, spiritually—in the direction of what we ask questions about.* Inquiry intervenes and it works both ways; it intervenes "inside" as well as "out there." In other words the questions we ask have a double import.

Now an honest admission. We wish that we too could enter into every new meeting, dinner conversation, or client contact with this feeling of profound wonder, of an opening to question new possibilities, or of what William James so aptly called, the state of "ontological wonder." But we do not. So how do we cultivate it? What we increasingly realize, again, is that it is all in the questions—the appreciative, life-centric ones, what we have called *the unconditional positive question.* The doorway into wonder may not be as narrow as it seems. Pragmatically, at least for us, it is not so much a process of trying romantically to recover the state of being a child; nor is it the same path taken by the mystic in spiritual retreat. Indeed, it can begin quite easily in ordinary circumstances of discovery, conversation, and the deepening of relationship, all endowed by the positive question.

**The Crux Of The Story**

Inquiry itself creates wonder. It is not the other way around. When we are really in a mode of inquiry, doorways into appreciable worlds open all around us. Entering into those worlds does not happen without questions. When we begin with genuine curiosity and inquiry, the feeling of wonder is the outcome. We know that we are doing inquiry when, at the end of the day, we feel wonder.

Chapter 9

# Building Community Capacity: AI With The US Navy

One of the most important developments in our approaches to organizational change using Appreciative Inquiry has been to challenge the status quo that strategic planning is best done in a select group of 15-20 key executives. Is it possible to do strategic planning with 60 people? How about 250? 1000? 5,000? Indeed, are we limiting the cooperative capacity of human systems to mobilize around a shared vision if we only tend to help small executive groups develop that vision? With the advent of large group interventions, we took Marvin Weisbord's call to "get the whole system in the room" seriously. A few of us who had been involved with the development of AI were inspired by this proposal and began to design events that included large groups. We continue to experiment with large group events in organizations from both the private and public sector, including The United Religions Initiative, GTE, Nutrimental, Roadway Express, World Vision, UN Global Compact, Bank of America, and the US Navy. This chapter shares a story about a long term engagement within the United States Navy. We choose to share it here partly to convey that if this process can build cooperative capacity in a command-and-control environment like the military, it can help everywhere!

**The Power of Working with the Whole**
While we are still in the experimental stages with applying large group methods and appreciative methods through what we call "AI Summits,"[31] we are already witnessing the power of whole system approaches to positive change. We have seen an exploding interest among change agents in experiments in large group interventions. In the authors' experiments facilitating summits, we have worked with groups ranging from 60 to nearly 5000 for three to four days.

We have seen, in fact, a transformation occur when the "whole system" is assembled or represented in the room. Various stakeholder voices are gathered together in real time conversations; each individual is invited to share his or her perspective and hear about experiences and views of others, unleashing new action possibilities that might have gone unimagined.

As we will see in the story that follows,[32] what we are calling the AI Summit also encourages the inclusion of external stakeholders, such as customers and suppliers. We hypothesize that *the design decision to include multiple and diverse voices is the catalyst that leads to a change in mindset because people then have access to an integral image of wholeness that transcends their well-learned routines.* Habits are interrupted so that expansive and inclusive scenarios can be proposed. The more that we can design a process that privileges every voice and that allows participants to see the emergence of the whole relational fabric of the firm, the more participants are pulled to contribute their best thinking. At a basic level, it is simply harder to maintain negative stereotypes of co-workers or the customer or the supplier when these parties are in the room, talking about their best experiences, and their highest hopes. Participants engaged in generative conversations that focus on what would benefit the entire system are able to discover and experience directly a common sense of purpose and direction.

The opportunity to hold or facilitate multiple AI summits in the same organization is a luxury that holds many potential lessons about the process of effective organization change. During the last two years, the authors have seen dramatic results as the Navy has used AI to develop and promote positive change in various parts of the system, including overall leadership development, fleet operations, family support services, the reserve force, the supply corps, the information professional community, and on board select ship communities. One of the most exciting and promising of these stories is our work with the Navy Information Professional (IP) Community, where we conducted two "summits" spaced ten months apart. These were large group, multiple stakeholder interventions to launch rapid, simultaneous, and self-directed improvements in a particular community within the Navy. The story of their first Summit follows.

## The Setting

As part of the Navy's structure, communities of practice allow sailors and officers to organize around a functional area of expertise. For example, the Aviation Community is responsible for ensuring that all pilots and related aviation officers receive proper training and are in a state of readiness. Similarly, the Submariner Community, Surface Warfare Community, and Human Resources Community provide their own specialized services throughout the Navy. The Information Professional (IP) Community is one of the newest of these functional areas.

The IP Community was officially organized as a new warfare community in October 2001. The Chief of Naval Operations (CNO) and the Navy's top uniformed officer, Admiral Vern Clark, issued a challenge for this community to "own the network" for the Navy and to increase the Navy's "network centric" capability as an integral, systematic strategic advantage.

## The Challenge

For the IP Community, the CNO's vision was a serious challenge. Members of the new Community had never experienced a strong sense of identity with other information professionals. Moreover, many of its members had struggled to find their place in the Navy at all. Traditionally, information technology specialists were seen as supporting the "real navy" who were deployed at sea. These factors led to a general atmosphere in which members of this Community consistently received subtle messages from their counterparts that they weren't quite as good as others in the Navy. In sum, to reach the CNO's vision, the IP Community needed to overcome these issues of identity, while developing stronger bonds with each other and the rest of the Navy.

Admiral Clark selected a three-star Vice Admiral, VADM Richard Mayo, to become the "Community Sponsor." As their advocate, this admiral specifically sought to help the IP Community develop a shared sense of purpose and identity. One of the Community members had learned about Appreciative Inquiry through Frank Barrett's work at the Naval Postgraduate School's Center for Positive Change in Monterey, California. After learning more, it was decided to use AI as the IP Community's vehicle for forging an identity, generating a sense of mission, and creating a strategy for moving into the future.

**The First Summit (2002)**
The first summit, held in September 2002, marked an important milestone in the development of the IP Community. Coming from deployments across the globe, IP officers forged new relationships, often meeting one another for the first time. The affirmative topic for the 2002 Summit, created with an executive steering group of 18 including several representatives from various fleet commands and a variety of ranks, was "The Information Power Advantage: Forge Information Dominance, Lead the Evolution of the Warfighter, and Open Portals for Innovation." About 170 of the 365 IP Community officers and about 80 external stakeholders attended.

Our overall design for the Summit followed the activities of the 4-D Cycle (see Chapter 6), conducted over three and one half days. During *Discovery*, we used appreciative interviews, stakeholder discussions about their "positive core," and the creation of pennants to identify and highlight the Community's greatest strengths. In the *Dream* phase they explored creative presentations of their ideal images for the IP Community, followed by the creation of an opportunity map with over 70 original ideas, to make the transition to the *Design* phase. After voting on their top four choices among the 67 ideas, Summit members self-selected into one of thirteen action groups. They self-organized by developing three-year Aspiration Statements, designating senior and junior "facilitator pairs," and by developing action plans for continued work after the Summit.

We observed several interesting dynamics during this Summit. First, most of the members of the Community were initially very curious, even somewhat anxious, about their participation. This anxiety extended even to the admiral responsible for creating this new IP Community who later reported that he had not slept well on the night before the Summit, unsure of what would happen with 250 people meeting for four days. However, by the end of the Summit, and for many months later, he reported, "That was my best week in the Navy." We heard echoes of his sentiment from many others as well.

Second, Community members engaged in self-organizing outside of the Summit structure. Many members of the Community were meeting for the first time and took advantage of this opportunity to establish or enhance interest groups. Several officer groups held separate meetings, often informally, to discuss their perspectives on Community efforts and the Community direction. In addition, while a sub-group clustered the opportunity map ideas, almost all of the remaining Summit participants held a spontaneous Town Hall Meeting, where they discussed more ideas for organizing and other issues of concern to Community members.

We also noted that much of the inquiry throughout the process focused on identity issues: "Who are we?" "How do we fit in with the rest of the Navy?" "What is our strategic importance to the Navy?" "How will we get recognition?" The Summit provided a venue for them to discover things about themselves that they often found surprising: they discovered a capacity for leadership and mentorship; they heard stories of IP Officers making a difference "at sea;" they created portrayals of a future where they were respected by others in the Navy, and where they experienced a high sense of professional competence. And most important, they heard numerous stories and comments from their leaders and other external stakeholders about their vital importance to the Navy and its mission. The specific topics from the Summit action teams, are illustrated below.

### First Summit Action Teams

*Career and Community Member Development (Defining who we are)\**

**Career Development\*\*** (one team for each area):

o   Career path

o   Certification for specific jobs

o   New member orientation and professional development

o   Professional development for existing IP Community members.

**Mentoring**: Developing a formal IP Officer mentoring program

*Marketing (Help others know who we are)*

**IP Community mission**: Define the overall purpose of the IP Community.

**Marketing**: Reach out to other Communities and IP members not in attendance.

**Virtual Workplace**: Refine the Community's online engagement capability.

*Information Dominance (Define who we are in relation to others)*

**Operational Relevance** (one team for each area):

o   Partnering with other Communities and Commands

o   Transitioning to the management of information and knowledge as a strategic advantage

o   Defining the IP role in the expeditionary strike group (battle groups)

**Innovation**: Develop initiatives to promote and share innovations

**Fellowship and Exchange**: Establish partnerships with civilian organizations

\* *Italics* represent cluster titles developed in a 3-month post-Summit follow-up meeting with team representatives

\*\* **Bold** represents team change topics developed from the Opportunity Map during the Summit.

Many participants left the Summit feeling energized about the possibilities and work that lay ahead. As one person stated in an open space at the conclusion, "I actually like being part of the Navy, today, right now. I'm really excited about what has happened here."

## Post Summit Work

We conducted a series of interviews with action group facilitators in November 2002 to follow up on the IP Community's Summit progress. In December 2002, a virtual teleconference was held with representatives from each of the 13 action groups. This same group convened an additional face-to-face meeting in February 2003 to follow-up and to regroup.

Many initial successes were noted at these meetings. At the February meeting, it was noted that the number of sea assignments (billets) had increased by over 300 percent and that many Fleet Commanders were now specifically requesting IP Officers. These observations suggested that the reputation of the IP Community was growing and that the Summit was having a wide-ranging effect. In addition, several core success factors were identified:

- *Support from Senior Leadership.* All successful pilot groups indicated that they have had strong involvement from senior officer leadership, even if this involvement is brief.
- *Frequent Communication.* All the successful groups had devised ways to work around the inherent limitations of geographical and technological distance.
- *Synergy with Regular Responsibilities.* Several facilitators suggested that their ability to contribute was aided when their regular duties already related to the pilot project.
- *Unambiguous Task Lists.* Successful groups had defined their milestones as clear actions rather than as more elusive steps such as "defining what needs to be done."

The pilot change teams relied on a lot of virtual teaming, since most of each team's members came from different commands and locations. We sought out what was working best for them and found supporting research in the management literature. These lessons became guidelines for this and future work via virtual teaming:

- *Match the form of communication to the degree of task and relationship complexity.* The more complex the task or relationships in a team, the greater the need for richer forms of communication such as phone conference, virtual teleconference or even face-to-face meetings.
- *Plan a rhythm of regular meetings with rich communication.* Regular meetings are like a heartbeat for a team. In a virtual environment, a routine of meetings drives the action.
- *Remove the anonymity from communication to maximize impact and response.* In a virtual environment, mass requests for a response are anonymous. Research indicates that anonymity feeds a norm of non-responsiveness.

In an effort to address emerging challenges, utilize best practices so far, and to capitalize on ideas above, the action team facilitators reorganized during their February face-to-face meeting. They combined the thirteen teams into three larger groups (information dominance, marketin, and career development), incorporating their goals into the three areas of focus outlined in the box above. This allowed them to make sure that they tackled their most pressing issues. They agreed to schedules of regular meeting times and created new guidelines for communication of anything related to the Summit on their Community web space.

Next, taking seriously the idea of establishing a "rhythm" for regular and intense interaction, they organized a "Community Executive Steering Group," (ESG) composed of 14 individuals representing a cross-section of the IP Community and relevant external parties. This ESG began meeting via phone conference every six weeks. At each meeting the action groups' facilitators submitted progress reports to the ESG, which became the clearinghouse for action items and milestones. In essence, by establishing a Community leadership committee, they created a venue for pumping life into the action groups *and* other programs/projects aimed at Community-wide issues.

Finally, they reconfirmed a decision to hold a second summit during July 2003, where they would specifically invite the IP Community members who had not attended the 2002 Summit. Everyone in the Community would be invited to attend the second Summit, but the goal was to make sure that all IP Officers would have at least one AI Summit experience. The second Summit was held with nearly 50% of the attendees representing various external stakeholders. The IP Community, now the center of the Network Warfare Command, is an integral part of Sea Power 21, the Navy's long-term future strategic plan.

In summary, what could have been a deficit-driven beginning of a new professional Community pre-occupied with an assumed negative perception of its personnel, became an exciting birthing process by partnering with the external stake-holders — or customers — of the Community through a series of large group, whole-system AI Summits. By convening these varied stakeholders and creating conversations based on perceived strengths and opportunities, the AI process ensured that common ground was discovered in relation to core strengths, preferred futures, and priority change initiatives. This commonness became the fabric for the newly formed IP Community and fueled the IP Professionals' capacity to partner with the Fleet and other naval commands desiring their services.

**FOCUS BOX**

The AI Summit provides a way for everyone to experience the whole system. By connecting strategic changes to the positive core, generated by all stakeholders, members are drawn to a preferred positive future that excites and energizes them to initiate new cooperation across institutional boundaries. In this case, the new IP Community transformed their "story" from one of low esteem, predicted infighting, and a 'second class' self-image to become a recognized and valued contributor to the Navy's overall mission. They are now leaders and expert owners of the Information Power Advantage; a strategic pillar in the Navy's long-term vision.

**Chapter 10**

# Conclusion: AI As Learning That Builds Cooperative Capacity

We start this chapter with our words from the final chapter of our book, *Appreciative Inquiry and Organizational Transformation*:[33]

> *Appreciative Inquiry's assumptions are generous; experiences with AI signal the power of holding affirmative beliefs about human systems. Our work with, and our colleagues' reports of, appreciative interventions has led us to believe that humans have rich reservoirs of courage and the freedom to sustain belief in the profound goodness of human nature, the nurturing potential of relationships, and the creative power of collective action (p. 265).*

This stance is the onset of a learning journey that builds, among other things, cooperative capacity. In fact, this may be the *natural path* of anyone who chooses to act of his or her free will.[34] This stance constitutes open, non-judgmental listening and a curiosity to discover, which fuels bold dreaming that compels us to experiment, to pilot changes, and to engage with others in new ways. AI is inherently about creating *learning relationships that are generative*.

The experience of doing an Appreciative Inquiry with multiple stakeholders of the same system creates both positive affect and relational "knowing" that reveals shared, co-constructed realities; these social constructions in the form of provocative propositions or aspiration statements (see Chapter 6) then attract participants to find new ways to work together for a common purpose or dream.[35] Their cooperative capacity—their conversational skills and imaginative potential—is ignited and transformed.

It is this cooperative capacity that resides in every social system that we wish to "appreciate." To develop cooperative capacity so that it actually grows requires us to inquire into what it is so that we can understand what triggers capacity building, what sustains it and what expands opportunities for cooperative engagement. In this book we have put forward our experience-based belief that AI is a means to do this. In this brief conclusion we summarize the key ideas we hope the reader will continue to reflect upon.

**Once again: Why AI?**
We have observed that the opportunities for organizational learning—and therefore capacity building—are typically limited by traditional change management approaches and to what we have observed as the "Decide-Advocate-Defend" (DAD) cycle. This is where a small, select group (usually at the top of a hierarchy) is invited to consider some strategic possibilities or choices, or what needs to change in order to better adapt/compete in the future. This group does, indeed, usually learn. They often do improve their capacity to work as an effective executive or leadership team. They consider new information, they conduct analyses, they question, and they debate. However, once they have *Decided*, they typically approach everyone else in the system with the agenda to *Advocate* their newly learned position or decision. While advocating for something, there is little, if any real questioning. One is too busy "outthinking the other" or "anticipating the opposition." Those who may really be curious or have questions to raise or wish to dialogue are met with a monologue that is often impersonal and inflexible. Any pushback or attempt to change the script of the small group is met with a *Defense*. The small group of "champions" who have already completed their learning journey now focuses on defending their opinion, position or decision and the deficit discourse (see Chapter 3) begins: the group asks, or wonders, why are you so resistant; why can't you trust us; why aren't you interested in what's good for the company; why do you always disagree before you hear us out; and so on.

Such a defensive spiral does not support the powerful, affirmative questions that underlie AI (see Chapter 4). Any organizational learning that could build cooperative capacity has *ceased* and the experiences of this D-A-D dynamic leads to social constructions that feed the "what's wrong with the leadership?" or "it's just another power play" kinds of stories. These quickly become strong memories that cause negative associations with any future change programs, strategic planning efforts, or visioning processes.

One might argue that there is some learning going on in the D-A-D cycle, but it is not the generative kind of co-discovery and co-creation that we have witnessed in AI processes. To remind ourselves of those capacity-building outcomes from an AI process, we turn now to the key factors that "give life" to these *generative learning relationships* that build cooperative capacity.

**The Magnetism of Experiencing Wholeness**
Whether it be a family, a sales team, a division of a global company, or a community, AI emphasizes getting all relevant stakeholder voices together in a representation of the entire system, if not literally *the* whole system. Through sharing stories and discovering the system's positive core, there is an "appreciative space" that develops revealing the core values and importance of the organization's identity. The appreciative stories revealed in the Discovery Phase (see Chapter 6) are generative experiences that call people to reflect upon the meaning of relationship, courage, wisdom, and innovation. They reveal the seeds of metaphors (see Chapter 8) that symbolize and encompass both the proud past and the possible future.

Through appreciative stories, the positive core of strengths generated from multiple voices and stories takes on a degree of sacredness—something to be honored, revered, nurtured, and protected. In an appreciative relational space such as this, where two or a thousand may be engaged, the image of the "whole" begins to take on a presence. When we have had the honor and opportunity to design and facilitate AI Summits (see Chapters 6 and 9) in systems like the US Navy, Roadway Express, UN Global Compact, and World Vision, we are repeatedly struck with the observation that something very special occurs when multiple stakeholders are able to simultaneously experience each other—seeing and feeling the most positive aspects of the "whole" of the organization or system in one room. *Relating to images of wholeness brings out the best in people.*

> *Elaboration of the positive core of a group or system creates a relational space that encourages learning by experimentation and further exploration of possibility. The simultaneous experience of positive affect generates real interest in shared possibilities.*

### Suspension of Habit through an Appreciative Disruption of Certainty

Learning what has the potential to transform an organization's capacity includes imagination, improvisation, and innovative thought. These are outcomes that are not likely to emerge from habitual deductive reasoning—the engine of problem-solving. AI creates relational spaces where curiosity reigns, where new possibilities are considered and embraced. The notion of "psychological safety" suggests that we least expect or desire such suspension of the comfortable (rational) status quo when we gather with people from other functions, constituencies, regions, and nationalities—people with whom we have had less frequent contact and therefore less relatedness. Yet our work with AI Summits, in particular, suggests this assumption about "stranger" or mixed stakeholder settings may be simply a myth.

The AI process enables a forklift operator and regional vice-president at Roadway Express who have never spoken to each other to engage immediately in a generative relationship that begins with the sharing of stories, mutual probing for underlying commonalities, and ends with imagined futures and action planning *together*. We have witnessed the same phenomenon with a young Navy recruit working with an admiral or a Thai staff worker in a children's relief project in Bangkok working with a wealthy donor living in North America. There is no reason to doubt that parties coming from different functions, different priorities, different agendas, different languages, and different operating norms can nonetheless discover common wisdom, common connection, common hope, and common purpose. When given the opportunity to share and find connections in what means most to us, human potentials are exposed and goodness is experienced. This is why in the Discovery phase of AI, stories about the "best moments" or highpoints related to any strategic topic (extraordinary teamwork, high margins, customer excitement, etc.) *always* reveal episodes of human cooperation. *Whatever "gives life" to the greatness of a human system will reveal cooperative capacity.*

**Cooperative capacity is fostered through an appreciative declaration of faith in the potential goodness of human groups and organizations.**

### Suspension of Hierarchy through Storytelling
Perhaps the largest barrier to building cooperative capacity in social systems is hierarchy. It is also, arguably, a necessary condition for any organizational form, flat or steep, where there needs to be some chain of responsible decision-makers to exercise authority for efficiency and effectiveness. Some situations definitely require chain-of-command and hierarchical modes of governance. However, traditional hierarchical modes of management can also block people from expressing good ideas, from fully understanding their roles, and from feeling a sense of ownership in shared goals. A hierarchy of persons implies a hierarchy of ideas, opinions, and knowledge. The expectation that others know more because of their position or because they control resources that impact the quality of the work life hinders the sharing of ideas or questions that may challenge the status quo. Hierarchy blocks inquiry and inquiry is essential to building or developing capacity to cooperate in creative organizational acts.

A common thread in all work with AI is the solicitation of stories about "best past" experiences in relation to the specific strategic topic under inquiry. Care is taken during AI sessions to remove normal symbols of rank, status, and parochial identity: only first names on ID badges; no uniforms in a military audience; no country or regional designations in a global gathering. While stories are being told, listeners are encouraged to actively help "mine for the gold" in the tales; to join in a mutual exploration of underlying causal factors and tacit lessons embedded in the stories. Such conversations value the storyteller's voice while searching for common ground. Being heard and having one's story actively analyzed in search of common success factors is empowering. It instills confidence and draws one into the relationship happening in the moment. This is the relational space in which possibilities can be explored without prejudice and where dependence on an expert does not hinder participation and engagement. *Co-construction* of innovative proposals is now possible.

> *Through storytelling, members create and communicate the moral structure, the sense of what is good and worth upholding, and the themes that create a sense of shared identity. A co-constructed identity founded on these factors is courageous, cooperative, and contagious.*

### A Final Message for Leaders: Positive Questions Beget Positive Action

As Peter Drucker suggested to our colleague, David Cooperrider, in a recent interview and emphasized throughout his classic book, New Society,[36] the main job of leadership today (and for the future) is *to continuously align the organization's strengths such that its weaknesses become irrelevant.* AI is a process deeply rooted in this strength-based notion of change and development. The Discovery phase is centered on seeking and revealing the "positive core" of a system in relation to some strategic topic. It is a collective search for the very best in our shared experiences, accompanied by a deep analysis of what causes participants to be at their best in those moments. The Dream and Design phases then help craft positive anticipatory images that start changing behavior — immediately — through the construction of provocative propositions and aspiration statements. Actionable plans arising from core strengths and shared ideals are then aligned with these bold dreams.

*Beginning any work activity with a powerful question to connect people with their collective positive core—their strengths—will enhance the likelihood of transformational learning and positive change.*

## Conclusion

The Appreciative mode of learning and capacity building is an invitation to change the way we think about change. More specifically, it signals a positive revolution in changing-with-each-other that can occur in human systems of all types and sizes. Returning to the core distinctive characteristics of the AI process (see Chapter 2) we can now say with confidence that it is possible—moreover predictable—*that the cooperative capacity of human systems that is necessary for organization growth and transformation is expanded when our relational spaces with each other are: focused on strengths; oriented toward a search for new understanding; inclusive of multiple stakeholder voices; always collaborative; and striving to be generative.*

What we have learned over the past two decades, after hundreds of experiments, is that AI is a powerful, strength-based, and collaborative approach to facilitating organizational change and growth that is rapid, sustainable, and transformative. Returning to this chapter's opening, AI ignites this positive change because all humans do possess a "rich reservoir" of cooperative potential, waiting to be unleashed. The essence of building cooperative capacity in human systems is to put the spotlight and questions on the good work, the best outcomes, and the most attractive aspects in that system. People engaged in this inquiry will naturally and quickly connect with their most positive beliefs about human groups and their potential to work, grow, dream, and celebrate together. They will naturally seek ways to move in directions that allow for more and more of that potential to be realized. The system's capacity to cooperate around multiple initiatives will expand.

**Final Thoughts**

Perhaps the biggest new message to take away from this very small book is that in any kind of contemporary human system it is both feasible and beneficial to BRING EVERYONE INTO THE INNER CIRCLE OF STRATEGY. Through AI we enable any and every stakeholder or member to learn and understand what is good, necessary, and life-giving; making it possible for the entire system to grow and perform at its very best. Armed with that information, people are compelled to attend to the whole, to cooperate, and thus infect the system with increased cooperative capacity.

# Selected References

## Recent Books
Theory and Practice:
Whitney, D. & Trosten-Bloom, A. (2003). *The Power of Appreciative Inquiry*. San Francisco: Berrett-Koehler.

Cooperrider, D. L., Whitney, D., and Stavros, J. M. (2003). *Appreciative Inquiry Handbook*. Bedford Hts., OH: Lakeshore Publishers.

Ludema, J. D., Whitney, D., Mohr, B. J. and Griffin, T. J. (2003). *The Appreciative Inquiry Summit*. San Francisco: Berrett-Koehler.

Watkins, J. M. and Mohr, B. J. (2001). *Appreciative Inquiry: Change at the Speed of Imagination*. San Francisco: Jossey-Bass/Pfeiffer.

Srivastva, S. and Cooperrider, D. L. (Eds.) (1999). *Appreciative Management and Leadership: The Power of Positive Thoughts and Action in Organizations*. Euclid, OH: Williams Custom Pub.

Case Studies:
Fry, R., Barrett, F., Seiling, J. and Whitney, D. (Eds.) (2000). *Appreciative Inquiry and Organizational Transformation: Reports from the field*. Westport, CT: Quorum.

Thatchenkery, T. (2005). *Appreciative Sharing of Knowledge: Leveraging Knowledge Management for Strategic Change*. Chagrin Falls, OH: Taos Institute Publishing.

## Websites
Resources for Appreciative Inquiry
   The Appreciative Inquiry Commons: http://ai.case.edu

Resources for Social Constructionist Thinking
   The Taos Institute: http://www.taosinstitute.net

**Appendix 1**

# Sample Summit Worksheets
# For the AI "4-D" Cycle

Excerpted from an AI Summit with Roadway Express

**Akron Roadway**

**Winning With Employee Driven Throughput:
Crushing non-union competition by delivering unsurpassed
speed and leveraging employee pride and involvement.**

Agenda Overview

**Day 1**
- Welcomes and Overview
- Introduction to TOPIC
- Community Building exercise

| | |
|---|---|
| ***Discovery:*** | 1:1 Appreciative Interviews<br>Mixed groups of Pairs search for themes and factors that "give life" to our TOPIC |
| | **Lunch** [Customer panel] |
| | Creating our shared History<br>Stakeholder groups: Identifying "proudest prouds" and what we want to keep |
| | Input: Where does Positive Change come from? |

- Summary and Close

211 Summit Agenda (continued):

**Day 2**
- Summarizing Key Success Factors and Practices to Preserve

---

*Dreaming*:    Mixed groups: Imagining possibilities for our TOPIC
Mapping Highest Impact Opportunities

Images of our Future around Opportunities of most Interest (in new, self-selected groups)

**Lunch**

Presentations of Images
Declaring Aspirations for the future:
3 yr. Goal and 1 yr. Steps

---

- Summary Reflections and Close

211 Summit Agenda (continued):

**Day 3**
- Summarizing our 3-year Aspirations

---

| | |
|---|---|
| *Design:* | Work on 1 yr. Targets and action steps<br>    Prepare presentation of "yes-able pro-<br>    posals for action"<br>Community Forum:<br>    Presentations from 3-4 Action Groups<br><br>**Lunch**<br><br>Presentations from 3-4 Action Groups |

---

| | |
|---|---|
| *Delivery:* | Team formation: Action Groups convene<br>    to agree on immediate next steps they<br>    will take next. |

---

- Personal commitments to act after this Summit

- "Open microphone" to entire community for comments/ reflections

- Close

**NOTE:** All sessions will begin and end on time. There will be breaks each morning and afternoon, with refreshments. All sessions will be videotaped so a summary of deliberations and action plans can be communicated (if we want) to the whole system.

## WHAT IS AN "AI" ORGANIZATIONAL SUMMIT?

*This is not your typical planning meeting!*

• The **WHOLE SYSTEM** participates—a cross-section of as many interested parties as is practical. That means more diversity and less hierarchy than is usual in a working meeting, and a chance for each person to be heard and to learn other ways of looking at the task at hand.

• Future scenarios—for an organization, community or issue—are put into **HISTORICAL** and **GLOBAL** perspective. That means thinking globally together before acting locally. This feature enhances shared understanding and greater commitment to act. It also increases range of potential actions.

• People **SELF-MANAGE** their work, and use **DIALOGUE**—not "problem-solving"—as the main tool. That means helping each other do the tasks and taking responsibility for our perceptions and actions.

• **COMMON GROUND** rather than "conflict management," is the frame of reference. That means honoring our differences rather than having to reconcile them.

• **APPRECIATIVE INQUIRY (AI)**— *To* **appreciate** means to value—to understand those things of value worth valuing. To **inquire** means to study, to ask questions, to search. **AI** is, therefore, a collaborative search to identify and understand the organization's strengths, its' potentials, the greatest opportunities, and people's hopes for the future.

• **COMMITMENT TO ACTION**—Because the "whole system" is involved it is easier to make more rapid decisions, and to make commitments to action in a public way—in an open way that everyone can support and help make happen.

## SELF-MANAGEMENT and
## GROUP LEADERSHIP ROLES

Each small group manages its own discussion, data, time, and reports. Here are useful roles for self-managing this work. **Leadership roles can be rotated.** Divide up the work as you wish:

• **DISCUSSION LEADER**—Assures that each person who wants to speak is heard within time available. Keeps group on track to finish on time.

• **TIMEKEEPER**—Keeps group aware of time left. Monitors report-outs and signals time remaining to person talking.

• **RECORDER**—Writes group's output on flip charts, using speaker's words. Asks person to restate long ideas briefly.

• **REPORTER**—Delivers report to large group in time allotted.

## Interview Conversations
(Turn to person next to you...completed by _____ o'clock)

**Our current reality.** Today's transportation environment is characterized by fierce competition in the 1 & 2 day regional markets. Everyday, we lose market share as current and former Roadway customers give more and more freight to non-traditional, non-union carriers who beat us at the game we "invented"—service! Why? How? Because they get the freight to destination faster than we do. We are better at rating bills and building high-n-tight claim-free loads. We have better computer systems and more dock doors. We have the best-trained and most skilled employees. On price, our base-rates are better than the regional carriers. Yet, they still beat us out of market share because they get the goods delivered quicker. But by leveraging the pride and involvement of our people, we can respond and recapture lost business...as well as establish new business. Our key to success in this arena is

### *Throughput*

Throughput represents how quickly we can process the freight through our facility. We win the battle for the 1 & 2 day market when we accelerate the processing of freight from pick-up, through the 211 gate, across the dock, and down the road. *System speed... that's our need.* If we can achieve maximum throughput, we will crush the non-union competition and we will dominate the market.

**Question 1:** Think back to a time at work that you recall as a "highpoint"...an experience or moment you remember as having left you with an intense sense of pride, excitement, or involvement in having been a part of something that was meaningful...a time that you truly felt you had contributed to the betterment of a fellow employee(s), the customer, or the organization.

Describe that experience; what was going on, who was involved, what made it so memorable?

**Question 2:** Tell me about a time when you thought throughput (speed) was at its best at 211, or when you were involved in moving a shipment quickly through facility to final destination in order to meet a customer requirement.

Tell the story of what was going on—who was involved and what happened.

What did you do? What did you value most about your involvement in that story?

What do you value most about the contribution of others in that story?

**Question 3.** <u>Tomorrow's reality</u>. Imagine that you have awakened from a deep sleep and 3 years have passed. It is 2004 and the landscape of regional LTL is different. Roadway dominates the non-union regional carriers in the marketplace! Wall Street is buzzing over the dramatic success Roadway has had in the regional markets! Articles in *Transport Topics* describe how Roadway — by tapping into the pride and involvement of its employees — has leveraged a dramatic improvement in *speed* at the 211 complex! This muscular, yet agile system has catapulted Roadway Akron to the forefront in reducing costs while establishing unparalleled levels of customer service and employee satisfaction. For customers, it's now *imperative* that they do their 1 & 2 day regional business with 211/Akron! For employees, 211 is a place that they would rather work than any other place!

What happened to allow for this kind of success?

What part did you play in this success?

What 3 wishes do you have to help Akron Roadway reach and sustain this success?

**Discovery:**

**Discovering The Resources And Strengths
In This Community**

GROUP REPORTS WILL BEGIN AT _____ O'CLOCK

**Purpose:** To appreciate and welcome each other, and to learn about the special experiences, commitments, capabilities, and resources people bring to this conference.

**Self Manage:** Select a Recorder, Reporter, Timekeeper and Discussion Leader

1. Introduce the person you interviewed. Go around the table. Introduce your interview partner to the group and share one highlight from your interview (high point story and vision of Roadway).

2. Next—as a group, talk about (each person shares):
   • What interests or excites you about being here? What results are you hoping for?

   • From the stories you heard, what stands out as key factors or themes that cause "Effective Throughput with Unsurpassed Speed Driven by Employee Involvement" here at the Akron Complex?

3. Recorder/Reporter listens for and prepares a two minute summary on:
   • Hopes we have for this meeting and results we want

   • 3-5 Key Factors that "give life" to Throughput with Unsurpassed Speed Driven by Employee Pride and Involvement

**Discovery:**

**Root Causes Of Success:
When Are We Most Effective And Why?**

REPORTS ARE DUE AT _____ O'CLOCK

**Purpose:** To look at the things we are doing that we are most proud of, and to understand the things that create success and build competitive advantage.

**Self-manage:** Select a Reporter, Recorder, Timekeeper and Discussion Leader

1. On a flipchart, list what YOU and THIS STAKEHOLDER GROUP are doing—or have done—that you are most PROUD of in relationship to our task—Achieving Maximum Throughput with Unsurpassed Speed, Driven by Employee Involvement and Pride: "*We are most proud of....* "

2. Select your "PROUDEST PROUDS" and come up with 2 actual examples/stories of successful "high throughput moments"

NOTE: These might be stories you told or heard in your opening interviews in pairs this morning.

3. Now do an analysis of the 2 stories. Have someone tell the story and listen for patterns. *What were the root causes of success? What happened new or different? What was it about the people and customers? What was it about the work group? What was it about the organization (e.g. procedures, resources, equipment, leadership, communications, training, etc.)?*

4. *Recorder*: List 5-10 Root Causes of Success; Things we want to keep doing, or do even better, no matter what else changes...

5. *Reporter*: Prepare a 3-minute summary—choose one story to re-tell to the whole group, and review the list of the root causes of success.

**The Future Of Akron Roadway**

**Moving From Discovery To Dream**

**Mapping The Opportunities for Improvement**

SUMMARIES ARE DUE AT _____ O'CLOCK

**Purpose:** To begin to build a future you want—an Akron Roadway team that is truly dedicated to "Maximizing Throughput with Unsurpassed Speed, Driven by Employee Pride and Involvement"

**Self Manage:** Select a Discussion Leader, Recorder and Timekeeper

1. Share your wishes and dreams from the interviews you did yesterday morning (Question 3). Add in any ideas or thoughts about changes or improvements that you think will have a major impact on improving our Throughput.

2. Brainstorm a list of <u>Opportunities to Improve Throughput</u> at the Akron Complex.

3. As a group, choose the 3-5 opportunities you all believe will have the greatest impact on Throughput.

**The Future Of Akron Roadway**

**Dreaming The Future We Want**

**Ideal Future Scenarios**

PRESENTATIONS ARE DUE AT _____ O'CLOCK

**Purpose:** To imagine and define the future you want to work toward — an Akron Roadway team that is truly dedicated to "Crushing the non-union competition by maximizing Throughput with Unsurpassed Speed, driven by Employee Pride and Involvement."

**Self Manage:** Select a Discussion Leader, Recorder and Timekeeper

1. Put yourselves 3 years into the future. It is 2004. <u>Visualize the Akron Complex you really want,</u> from the perspective of the Opportunity Area you have chosen.
   - What is happening?
   - How did this come about; what helped it happen?
   - What are the things that support this Vision; leadership, structures, training, procedures, etc.?
   - What makes this Vision exciting to you?
   - How does this Vision maximize Throughput with Unsurpassed Speed?

2. Capture this Dream in a 3-year Aspiration Statement draft on 1 flipchart page: "By 2004, what we most aspire to in terms of <u>(your chosen opportunity area)</u>, is...." [See 2 Examples on next page]
   - Use vivid language
   - Be positive
   - Be bold, provocative...make it a stretch that will attract others

3. Choose a creative way to present your Vision to the rest of us in a <u>5-minute</u> "portrayal" as if it existed now — use as many members of your group as possible in the presentation.

Examples: * A TV News Report * A Song or Poem * A Day in the Life... * A Skit * A Hiring Interview * Etc.

**The Future Of Akron Roadway**

**Dreaming The Future We Want**

Example Aspiration Statements:

#1  Opportunity Area: Delegation & Trust
"Roadway 2003: Roadway is an organization that is world class in terms of its leaders developing leaders at all levels. We are known throughout the industry for our core competency of delegation. People want to work at Roadway because all employees are trusted and empowered to create value."

#2  Opportunity Area: Career Opportunity/Training/Mentoring
"Roadway is a proactive organization that enables employees to achieve their personal career goals by offering career opportunities, centrally administered and personally initiated training/education, with mentoring.

Career opportunities are provided by vehicles such as internal job fairs, intranet job postings, utilization of a skills database, career assessment inventories, and a formalized mentoring process with a key emphasis on promoting within.

All employees are provided time for various training where tuition reimbursement for continuing education is "boundaryless" (i.e. all depts., job levels, interest levels), fully supported, budgeted, and funded.

Training includes soft skills for all employees, leadership training, advanced technical training, while utilizing experienced personnel as a training asset."

## The Future Of Akron Roadway

## Designing For Optimal Throughput

**Purpose:** To begin translating your 3-year Aspiration Statement into 1-year goals and steps to be taken in the next 6-12 months

**Self Manage:** Select a Discussion Leader, Recorder, and Time-keeper

1. Using the feedback and comments from other groups, take 10-15 minutes to revise, edit, or improve on your Aspiration Statement.

2. Formulate 1-year goals that can be achieved and will demonstrate we are on our way to your 3-year Aspiration:

- Brainstorm ideas about specific things that can occur or be changed by 1 year from now that will put us on a course to realize your Vision for 2004

3.  Identify possible actions to achieve 1-year goals:

- Agree on key targets and scenarios for how to get there: Who would need to do what? By when?

   Guidelines for Goals and Action Steps:
   a.  Does it support our key business objectives?
   b.  Does it address/reflect the underlying principles in our Aspiration Statement?
   c.  What are we already doing (Key Success Factors from yesterday) that can be continued or enhanced?
   d.  What are new actions that would create an impact?
   e.  Can all stakeholders support the idea?

**Akron Roadway**
*Declaring The Future We Want*

**Delivering On Our Highest Hopes For The Future**

PRESENTATIONS ARE DUE AT _____ O'CLOCK

**Purpose:** To prepare and present your Opportunity Group's proposals for improving Throughput to achieve Unsurpassed Speed through Employee Pride and Involvement.

**Self Manage:** Select a discussion Leader, Recorder, Timekeeper and Reporter

1. Discuss and finalize your Group's Goals and Action Steps by addressing the items below. In the break before presentations, you will be able to transfer your work onto a set of Powerpoint slides for the presentation.

Points to Address and Include in your Presentation:
- o   Name of Opportunity Area your Group formed around and names of group members.
- o   Your 3-Year Aspiration Statement
- o   Your 1-Year Goals & Action Steps
- o   Expected Outcomes:
  - • What will this recommendation do for Throughput?
    - • What specific impact are you hoping for?
    - • How can we measure this?
- o   Building Commitment:
  - • Who will be most impacted by this?
  - • How can they be brought on board after this Summit?
- o   Sustaining Momentum
  - • What support do we need to implement our plans?
  - • What can we (this team) do immediately to get action going?

# Endnotes

1. Collins, J. (2001). *Good to Great*. New York: Harper Collins.

2. Listen to William Wallace describe the challenge Michelangelo faced: "Marble carving is hard work, loud and dirty. Every blow of hammer to chisel is a collision of metal against metal striking stone. Marble chips fly in all directions; the dust lies thick. Modern stone workers wear goggles; Michelangelo did not. He had to see the stone, to see each mark, to make tiny adjustments to the angle of his chisel and to the force of his blow. He could not afford to slip. One wrong stroke could break a finger, an arm, or worse. A figure comes alive only after thousands and thousands — tens of thousands — of perfectly directed hard and soft blows. Marble carving is difficult and unforgiving." (Wallace, William. (1998). *Michelangelo: The Complete Sculpture, Painting, Architecture*. Beaux Arts Edition).

3. Johnson, Paul. (2000). *The Renaissance: A short history*. New York: Modern Library.

4. Cameron, K. S., Dutton, J. E., & Quinn, R. E. (2003). Foundations of Positive Organizational Scholarship. K. S. Cameron, J. E. Dutton, & R. E. Quinn (eds.), *Positive Organizational Scholarship: Foundations of a new discipline* (pp. 3-13). San Francisco: Berrett Koehler.

5. Hall, T. (1998). Seeking a Focus on Joy in the Field of Psychology. *New York Times*, Science Desk, April 28.

6. Hamel, G. (2000). *Leading The Revolution*. New York: Penguin, 13-14.

7. Frederickson, B. L. (2003). The Value of Positive Emotion. *American Scientist*, 91, 330-335.

8. Argyris, C. (1987). A Leadership Dilemma: Skilled Incompetence. *Business and Economic Review*, 1 (1), 4-11.

9. Gergen, K. (1997). *Realities and Relationships*. Cambridge: Harvard University Press.

10. Sarbin, T. (ed) (1986). *Narrative Psychology: The Storied Nature of Human Conduct*. NY: Praeger Publishers.

11. Cooperrider, D. L., Barrett, F. & S. Srivastva (1995). Social Construction and Appreciative Inquiry: A Journey in Organizational Theory. In Hosking, D., Dachler, P. and Gergen, K. (eds.) *Management and Organization: Relational Alternatives to Individualism.* Aldershot: Avebury Press.

12. Gergen, K., McNamee, S. & F. Barrett (2001). Toward Transformational Dialogue. *International Journal of Public Administration.* 24.

13. Wittgenstein, L. (1961). *Tractatus Logico-Philosophicus,* D. F. Pears and B. F. McGuinness (trans.), New York: Humanities Press.

14. Cooperrider, D. L. and Whitney, D. (2000). A Positive Revolution in Change: Appreciative Inquiry. In Cooperrider, D. L., Sorensen, P., Whitney, D., & T. Yeager (eds.). *Appreciative Inquiry.* Champaign, IL: Stipes, 7-8.

15. Heidegger, M. (1927). *Being and Time.* New York: Harper and Row.

16. Boulding, E. (1988). *Building a Global Civic Culture.* Syracuse University: Syracuse Studies on Peace and Resolution Press.

17. Ludema, J., Cooperrider, D. L., Barrett, F. (2000). Appreciative Inquiry: The Power of the Unconditional Positive Question. In Reason, P. and Bradbury, H. (eds.) *Handbook of Action Research.* London: Sage Press.

18. Fry, R., Barrett, F., Seiling, J., Whitney, D. (eds.) (2000). *Appreciative Inquiry and Organizational Transformation: Reports from the Field.* Westport, CT: Quorum.

19. Sarbin, T. (ed.) (1986). *Narrative Psychology: The Storied Nature of Human Conduct.* New York: Praeger.

20. Collins, J. and Porras, J. I. (1994). *Built To Last: Successful Habits of Visionary Companies.* New York: Harper Business.

21. Video. (1993). *Speed, Simplicity and Self-Confidence: Jack Welch Speaks with Warren Bennis.*

22. Cooperrider, D.L. and Whitney, D. (1999). *Collaborating for Change: Appreciative Inquiry.* San Francisco: Berrett-Koehler.

23. Now a business unit of Yellow-Roadway after merger in 2003.

24. There is a basic format to these AI questions. For more guidance, see Cooperrider, D. L., Whitney, D. and Stavros, J. M. (2003). *The Appreciative Inquiry Handbook*. Bedford Hts. Ohio: Lakeshore Publishers.

25. *Ibid.*

26. Barrett, F. (1995). Creating Appreciative Learning Cultures. *Organization Dynamics*. 24, 36-49.

27. For more information on the British Airways story, see Cooperrider, D. L., Whitney, D., Stavros, J. (2003). *The Appreciative Inquiry Handbook*. Bedford Heights, OH: Lakeshore Publishers.

28. Barrett, F. & Cooperrider, D. L. (1990). Generative Metaphor Intervention. Journal of Applied Behavioral Science, 26, 219-239.

29. Barrett, F. J. (1990). The Development of the Cognitive Organization. (Doctoral Dissertation, Case Western Reserve University). UMI, No. 9021373.

30. *Ibid.*

31. Ludema, J. D., Whitney, D., Mohr, B. J. & T.J. Griffin. (2003). *The Appreciative Inquiry Summit*. San Francisco: Berrett-Koehler.

32. We wish to acknowledge David Bright, an advanced doctoral student at Case Western Reserve University who helped the authors facilitate this AI Summit and assisted in the case write-up.

33. Fry, R. and Barrett, F. (2000). Conclusion: Rethinking What Gives Life to Positive Change. In Fry, R., Barrett, F., Seiling, J., Whitney, D. (eds). *Appreciative Inquiry and Organizational Transformation: Report from the field*. Westport, CT: Quorum, 263-278.

34. Barnard, C. (1968). *The Functions of the Executive*. Cambridge: Harvard University Press.

35. Gergen, K. (1994). *Realities and Relationships: Soundings in social construction*. Cambridge: Harvard University Press.

36. Drucker, P. (1993). *New Society: The Anatomy of Industrial Order*. Transaction Publishers.

# About The Authors

**Frank J. Barrett** is Associate Professor of Management and Organizational Behavior at the Naval Postgraduate School, Monterey, California. He is also on the faculty of Human and Organizational Development at the Fielding Graduate Institute. His doctoral degree is from Case Western Reserve University where he worked with David Cooperrider and Suresh Srivastva and was part of the group that originated the theory and practice of Appreciative Inquiry. He has published numerous articles on topics in organizational change and learning, appreciative inquiry, and organizational design as improvisation. Frank currently directs the Center for Positive Change at the Naval Postgraduate School. He has coauthored with David Cooperrider an award winning paper: "Generative Metaphor Intervention." He is also an active jazz pianist. His email address is: fbarrett@cruzio.com.

**Ronald E. Fry** is Associate Professor of Organizational Behavior at Case Western Reserve University in Cleveland, Ohio where he has directed the Weatherhead School of Management's internationally recognized Executive MBA program for the past 15 years. He has recently become the director of Case's new Masters Program in Positive Organization Development and Change. Ron was also part of the group at Case that originated the theory and practice of AI and currently teaches with his colleague, David Cooperrider, a Certificate Program in Appreciative Inquiry for the Benefit of Business and Society. Ron has published widely on team development, executive leadership, organizational change and appreciative inquiry. He also directs the Institute for Advancements in AI as part of Case's new Center for Business as an Agent for World Benefit.

CPSIA information can be obtained
at www.ICGtesting.com
Printed in the USA
BVHW04s1317290818
525950BV00016B/129/P